W. DANIEL QUILLEN

Beginner's Guide to Genealogy

Essential Tools, Records, and Techniques For Beginning Genealogists

First published by Sprint Publishing 2023

Copyright © 2023 by W. Daniel Quillen

All rights reserved. No part of this publication may be reproduced, stored or transmitted in any form or by any means, electronic, mechanical, photocopying, recording, scanning, or otherwise without written permission from the publisher. It is illegal to copy this book, post it to a website, or distribute it by any other means without permission.

W. Daniel Quillen has no responsibility for the persistence or accuracy of URLs for external or third-party Internet Websites referred to in this publication and does not guarantee that any content on such Websites is, or will remain, accurate or appropriate.

First edition

This book was professionally typeset on Reedsy.
Find out more at reedsy.com

Contents

1	Introduction	1
2	Why Genealogy?	3
3	Getting Started	5
4	Vital Records	13
5	What's in a Name?	20
6	Census Records	29
7	Military Records	56
8	Immigration and Naturalization Records	67
9	Using the Church of Jesus Christ of Latter-day Saints	77
10	Genealogy Societies	88
11	Tools of the Trade – The Internet	96
12	Genealogy Software	101
13	Help Your Descendants — Write a Personal History and Keep a...	104
14	Kids & Genealogy	118
15	Chat Generative Pre-Trained Transformer (ChatGPT)	125
16	In Summary	131
17	Resources	133
18	Praise for Quillen's Other Genealogy Books	135
19	Quillen's Other Books	137
20	About the Author	138

1

Introduction

Welcome to the World of Genealogy. I may be biased, but I think you are going to really enjoy this new adventure!

I'm not going to lie — Genealogy is a hobby that can consume you. You'll find it as addictive as eating your favorite potato chips. There will be times when you will spend many hours in pursuit of your ancestors, but then there will be other times when you rest from your genealogical labors for a bit (like weeks or even months). But like a good friend (or family member!), you can easily pick up where you left off and start out again.

Through the pages of this guide, I'll show you the basic skills, records and websites you need to begin your genealogical journey – techniques to use, records to find, and how to find them. While much of the information and records I provide will be basic, I'll weave in a few professional genealogists' secrets as well.

Because I've made many mistakes in my quest to find my ancestors through the years, I have had to learn the hard way. You'll find warnings about many of those mistakes I made (and had to correct) throughout the pages of this book.

But at the end of the day – this is a book for beginners and focuses on the basics. I've written eight other genealogy books that go further in-depth on these topics I'm sharing with you in this book, but I want you to have a sound, sturdy foundation as you begin your ancestral research. So – let's go have some fun.

2

Why Genealogy?

Why is genealogy so popular? Many societies – Asian, Native American, African and others — kept accurate and extensive genealogies that extended back for hundreds, even thousands of years. Many of them were kept in the memories of tribal Elders and passed on in the oral tradition, spiced with stories of heroism and tragedy from the lives of their forbears.

One might even argue (successfully, I think), that the dusty hobby/livelihood of archaeology is nothing more than an effort to find man's earliest roots – in other words — genealogy!

Nearly since the birth of the United States, Americans have been interested in who they were and where they came from. A mere fourteen years after the signing of the Declaration of Independence, the first census of the United States was commissioned by Congress, and censuses have continued unabated every decade since that time. Our Founding Fathers weren't merely interested in counting the people. The earliest US censuses counted families. They listed the names of heads of households, as well as the age ranges of members of the family and their sex. Since that time, the census instrument has been refined to provide us with great detail on the lives of our progenitors – names, age, sex, number of children, occupation, home owner or renter, and the state or country of the individual's parents' birth.

Before you set out on your genealogical journey, let's set one thing straight. The hobby you are involved in is spelled GeneAlogy, not GeneOlogy. That third syllable, however, can be pronounced either like al or awl – it makes no difference. But if you are going to pick up genealogy as a hobby, let's make sure you spell it correctly!

3

Getting Started

At this point, you may find yourself wanting to ask me: "So Dan, I've got this – genealogy can be a lot of fun, and it can be an obsession. You've captured my attention. But what I want to know is: What skills and information do I *really* need to get started in this intriguing venture?"

To which I would respond:

- "You need to have an interest in learning more about your ancestors.
- You need to know what kinds of records exist that might provide information about them.
- You need good Internet search tools to help you find ancestral records. As your primary search tools, I suggest Ancestry.com, FamilySearch.org, and MyHeritage.com. But don't forget Google!
- You need to know the techniques you need to employ to find your ancestors.
- Perhaps the most important thing you need is to learn how to be a detective – you will run into many blind alleyways in search of your ancestors, and you'll need to be able to reason out how else you might find these elusive ancestors of yours.

- And finally – you need patience and joy in The Chase. Patience to persevere when these ancestors keep slipping away, just out of your grasp. And joy at finally cornering and capturing them."

And – it's all worth it!

Where to Begin?

So where *do* you begin? The quickest and easiest way to get started in your genealogical quest is easy – start with yourself and your immediate family. What do you already know about yourself, your parents, grandparents, and even great grandparents? If you already know a lot – good for you. If not, then ask those closest to you about those who have gone beyond.

Your parents are a good place to start. They'll know their parents' names (your grandparents), and probably their birthdates and birthplaces. Write that information down. My grandparents were born five decades before me. I was fortunate enough to know them and could get information directly from them…and then they provided me with information about several of my great grandparents – who were born between 75 and 90 years before me.

Ask your parents (as well as your Aunt Ruth, or Uncle Jim, or whoever else is still around) for as much information as you can – not only names, dates and places, but stories about your ancestors' lives. And write it all down – either in a handwritten genealogy journal / notebook, or perhaps in a file on your computer. But capture all the information you can.

Then, try and find out if they have birth and marriage certificates, death certificates, and so forth. Sometimes those records provide invaluable information about those people, but also their parents. Church records, like baptismal and confirmation certificates, also provide a wealth of knowledge some times.

Old photographs frequently yield valuable information. Often, someone has written on the back of a picture: "Uncle Bud at Lake Texoma with two-year—old Jr., Summer 1943." Information like that can provide hints to unraveling your family history. In the summer of 1943, Little Jr. was two years old – so he must have been born in 1941 or thereabouts. And you may learn your uncle's name (Bud) was a childhood nickname he never outgrew.

Most genealogy guides suggest beginning with your parents. Obviously I agree with that, although I do so with one caveat. Almost every family I know of has someone – generally an older relative – who is considered the "family genealogist," or if not the family genealogist, the one person in the family who just seems to have an interest in and who remembers all the pertinent facts about the family. In my case, it was my Great Aunt Ruth, my grandfather's sister. Of all my extended relatives, she was the one who had the most interest in and knowledge of the history of the family.

If you have an "Aunt Ruth" in your family, then I suggest starting with her. If she lives in town or nearby, then arrange to meet her to talk about the family. If it is not practical because of distances, then the telephone is a wonderful genealogical tool. E-mail is a possibility, but I find most of the people from my grandfather's generation are not computer literate. Maybe even FaceTime if your Great Aunt Ruth is up to it, technologically speaking (or maybe one of her nearby kids or grandkids can lend a hand).

Other records that may be of assistance include old letters between family members, newspaper articles and obituaries, old family Bibles. The latter often contain valuable genealogical information.

Earlier, I mentioned you need some way to search the Internet for online records. My two personal favorites are Ancestry.com and FamilySearch.org. The former is a fee-based, subscription service ($130 to $300 per year subscription, depending on the package you select). FamilySearch is a free service, hosted by the Church of Jesus Christ of

Latter-day Saints. You do not have to be a member of their Church to use FamilySearch, but you do have to register. Both Ancestry and FamilySearch have access to billions of on-line ancestral records.

In your research, you may run across county and family histories and genealogies. I once found an online county history that included the biography of my fourth great grandfather, who was born in 1788 – when few vital records like birth, death, and marriage certificates were kept. It provided me with fabulous information about him, his parents (born in the mid-1700s), his wife and only son. It also provided information about his military career, and his military records allowed me to discover even more about this patriotic ancestor of mine.

Organization

As you begin your search, you need a method to store and organize information you find. In the "olden days," this would have been file folders with tabs for each family surname. You can still do that, but most of the people I know prefer to keep the information they find electronically, as they scan and save vital records in computer folders. Whichever format you use, the idea is the same: keep the information and records you have found in a place where you can easily access it – and document where you found them. Whether you use paper and hanging folders with family surnames on them, or create directories and folders on your computer, it doesn't make any difference – just keep the information you have found. And don't forget to keep information about where you found it – a URL, book, online county history, Ancestry.com or FamilySearch.org, etc.

The Language of Genealogy

As you venture into this exciting new world, you need to know that genealogy, like most other hobbies, has its own lingo. Below are a few terms you are likely to run into as you begin your research in earnest:

Family Group Sheet – this is a document that groups a family together under their father. Included will be a man, his wife and all of his children, along with important information about each person, such as their birth, marriage and death dates and places. It is one of the main forms used in genealogy research.

FamilySearch Center – genealogy libraries staffed by volunteers of the LDS Church where genealogists can access the LDS Church's vast genealogical records. They are open to any genealogist, regardless of religious persuasion. They are found in many local LDS Church buildings.

Maternal – used to describe which line of the family tree you are referring to. Your maternal grandfather is your mother's father.

Paternal – used to describe which line of the family tree you are referring to. Your paternal grandfather is your father's father.

Pedigree Chart – this is a chart the will show at a glance what your "family tree" looks like, by showing in graphic form who your parents, grandparents, great grandparents, etc., are. A limited amount of genealogical information is included. This too is an important genealogical form.

Primary Source – these are genealogy records created at the time of the event. A birth certificate would be considered an original record.

Secondary Source – genealogy records where information is provided much later than the event. A tombstone or death certificate would be considered a primary source for death information, but a secondary source for birth information, since it is likely the birth information was provided many years after the deceased person's birth occurred.

Vital Records – this is the term used to refer to records for an individual's birth, marriage and death.

You can record that information on a Family Group Sheet and/or a Pedigree Chart. There are a number of online places you can go to get free Family Group Sheet and free Pedigree Chart forms. One of the best places for forms I've found is at the National Genealogical Society. Their website is *NGSGenealogy.org*. Go there, and in the tray near the top, click on *Learning Center*, then in the drop-down box, select *Free Genealogy Resources*. You'll need to create a free account, and after that you can access their free fillable forms.

Okay – now it's time to learn a bit about how to find your ancestors in genealogical records.

PRECIOUS HISTORY DISCOVERED

In my role as family genealogist, I pestered my grandmother for years for information about her family. She shared a few small photos of her parents when they were in their 80s. After my grandmother's death, my parents went to Oklahoma to help my grandfather pack up the house so that he could move in with them in their home in Colorado.

While going through their personal effects of nearly 60 years of marriage, my parents discovered a box in their old Model T garage that contained perhaps 400 family photographs. Most of the pictures had been labeled by my great grandmother with the names of all individuals in the photo, and many photos included the date the photo was taken.

The photos were of several lines of our family, and I was able to match the information on the photos with the genealogy this great grandmother had written in the center section of the family Bible. It was a remarkable find, a precious discovery.

Getting Started Checklist

_____Gather together all the vital record sources you have found – certificates, photos, etc.

_____Decide on an organizational methodology (file cabinet, binders, computer folders, etc.)

_____Be sure and record where you found your ancestors' information – the URL, book, interview with a grandparent, or whatever.

_____Procure materials that will support your method of organization. (Notebook, hanging folder, computer, etc.)

_____As you gather information, write it down and then file it!

_____Familiarize yourself with forms that may assist you in organizing the genealogical information you collect. Free Family Group Sheets and Pedigree charts are available from NGSGenealogy.org.

_____Select the appropriate forms you need to match the information you have.

Additional Resources

Carmack, Sharon Debartolo, *Organizing Your Family History Search: Efficient & Effective Ways to Gather and Protect Your Genealogical Research*, Betterway Publications. (April 1999)

Dollarhide, William, *Managing a Genealogical Project*, Genealogical Publishing Company. (May 1999)

4

Vital Records

Vital records are those records that are critical to successful and accurate genealogical research. Every genealogist should strive to find original vital records for each ancestor they are researching. These original records provide information about the names, dates and places of births, marriages and deaths of those for whom you are searching.

These important and original records (by original, I consider photocopies or digital copies of the originals as good enough) will often shed a great deal of light on the family you are researching. I have seen birth certificates, for example, that contain some or all of the following information:

- Individual's full name
  - Birth date
  - Place of birth
  - Residence of parents
  - Mother's maiden name
  - Mother's age at the time of this birth
  - Number of children born previously to this mother

- Father's full name
- Father's age at the time of this birth
- Father's occupation
- State or country of origin of parents

Death certificates likewise contain some of the same information, adding the death date, cause of death and the spouse's name. Here is an example of such a death certificate of a distant cousin, which I was able to find on Ancestry.com:

Marriage certificates often provide just the basics: full names of the bride and groom and the date and place of the marriage. Marriage registers, however, often contain more information about the couple, including parents' names and the age of the bride and groom, and whether either the bride or groom had been married before (and to whom). Marriage registers were books that were kept by the local government (typically the county) of all marriages occurring within its boundaries.

Where to Look?

Once again, we turn to our friendly neighborhood genealogy website to locate this information. Most of the genealogy subscription services, and several of the free genealogical services, can open the Vital Records door wide for you. Let's see how FamilySearch can help you find Vital Records.

Let's use my father's parents as an example – Helon Quillen and Vivian Cunningham. **A genealogical tip to remember**: when you're looking for records for one of your female ancestors, if it's before she's married, you need to use her maiden name. I know that seems silly to mention it, but I have caught myself many times forgetting that tip and wondering why I couldn't find their birth or marriage record!

Let's say I want to find information about my grandparents' marriage. Login to FamilySearch. (If you've not created an account, you'll need to do that first. It will take a minute or two.)

From the home page, select *Search,* then in the drop-down box, select *Records.* A box will pop up asking for your ancestor's first names, last name, place, and the year of their birth or death. For my grandmother, I entered:

First names: Vivian Iris
   Last name: Cunningham
   Place; Norman, Oklahoma

Year (birth or death): 1906

When I hit *Return*, I received over 3,000 records that might be my grandmother (or might not be!). The most-likely ones should be listed first. In her case, there were census records, some school records, her death record, and many others. Scanning the list, the second one said: Marriage / Bride. That tells me that on this record she was married and listed as the bride (instead of mother, sister, witness, etc.) I clicked on that record and found this marriage license and certificate for my grandparents:

The whole process took less than one minute! I now have a copy of my grandparents' marriage record in less time that it took you to read about it.

Many birth, death, and marriage vital records are available online – now it's your turn. Select an ancestor you'd like to learn more about, and try it. Query FamilySearch.org for their birth, death or marriage information, and see what you can find!

If you're not going to use the Internet, locate the Vital Records department of the state or county where your ancestor's birth, death or marriage may have taken place. This may be found in on the Internet, or through a book written specifically for this purpose. If you decide to do that, be precise in your request, provide as much info as they will need to locate the records (for example – full name if you know it, approximate birth year or range of years, place, parents' names, etc.). Include a stamped, self addressed envelope and the current amount the government entity charges for their search.

My second great grandfather — William Lindsey McCollough

Vital Records Checklist

____Create a FamilySearch.org account, or an Ancestry.com account. The former is free, the latter has a subscription fee.

____Determine which ancestor you want to get information about.

____Gather the information you already know about this person

(name, place of birth, approximate birth year, etc.)

____Write a letter to the state's Vital Records Department, requesting the certificate you are looking for. Make sure to:

____Include a self-addressed, stamped envelope (SASE)

____Include a check or money order (never cash!) for the cost of the certificate.

____Be specific in your request.

____Do not request too many certificates at one time.

Additional Resources

Bentley, Elizabeth Petty, *The Genealogist's Address Book*, Genealogical Publishing Company. (February 1991)

Dollarhide, William, (Alice Eichholz, editor), *Ancestry's Red Book: American State, County and Town Sources,* Ancestry Publishing. (2004) (Though a little outdated, still a great resource to get you in the right place.)

Hansen, Holly, *Handy Book for Genealogists: United States of America*, Everton Publications, 11th edition. (2006)

Kemp, Thomas Jay, *International Vital Records Handbook*, Genealogical Publishing Company; (2017)

5

What's in a Name?

When I was growing up, one of my classmates was named Eric, and he had copper-colored bright red hair. On one occasion, our sixth-grade class was covering a unit on family history and we were each asked to find out about one of our ancestors, and prepare and present an oral report to the class. When the day came for Eric to make his report, he stood in front of the class, blushing to the bright-red tips of his freckled ears, and told us that one of his ancestors was Eric the Red, the intrepid Viking explorer....(yeah, right Eric!). As I recall, we had a pretty good laugh at Eric's expense. I never did find out if he was really a descendant of The Eric the Red!

I thought my friend Eric might have been kidding is, but then again, maybe he wasn't kidding. Little did I know then, that through the centuries many people were named after physical characteristics that they or a relative possessed. In fact, there is a wide variety of naming schemes that might give you a clue to something about your progenitors. Read on for a few thoughts on the topic.

Physical Characteristics

Many of those around us still carry the names of our progenitors that may have once reflected their physical characteristics. Ever know a person whose surname was Klein? Klein means small in German. How about Rubio (Spanish for blonde) or Blanco (Spanish for white)? Delgado means thin in Spanish, and the popular name Rojas may have been once used to identify a strain of the family with red hair (since rojas means red or rosy).

An Animal Connection

Many surnames reflect the names of animals. Perhaps an ancestor handled, raised or sold certain kinds of animals, or perhaps they were just fond of or admired a particular kind of animal. They may have even looked like a particular animal. Consider for example, the following: *Adler* (eagle in German), *Aguilar* (eagle in Spanish), *Haas* (rabbit in German) or *Garcia* (fox in Spanish) or *Fox* (also fox in English). Have you ever known someone named *Leon* (lion in Spanish) or perhaps *Faulkner* (falken is hawk in German)?

Patronymics

Many cultures employed the use of patronymics when taking names for themselves. A patronymic is a name that identifies the named person with his or her father.

The Irish had their own form of patronymics recognized the world over. Prefixes such as Mc or Mac were used to signify the *son of*: McDonnell was therefore the son of Donnell. Another prefix was the O' which meant "descended from," and a grandson or great grandson might use such a prefix. Occasionally the English passed laws to annoy the Irish (actually, they were trying to assimilate them into English culture). One such law forbade the use of the patronymics O' and Mc. At that time, the patronymic *fitz* replaced Mc for son of: Fitzmorris then meant the son of Morris.

Almost as prevalent as Irish patronymics are Scandinavian patronymics. I suppose we all know more than our fair share of individuals with surnames like Anderson (Anders' son) and Johnson (John's son). For centuries Scandinavians employed this naming scheme, and until surnames became common (in the late 1700s or early 1800s depending on the location), the names changed from generation to generation.

The Jewish culture also has its patronymics. You will occasionally see the name *ben* used to designate the son of, as in David *ben* Joseph (David, the son of Joseph). Certain Jewish groups also used patronymics to honor living grandparents, and there was a specific order used to designate names. The first-born son was often named after his paternal grandfather, and his brother (the second son) was named after his maternal grandfather. They used this practice for their daughters too: first-born daughters were given the name of their paternal grandmother and second-born daughters received the names of their maternal grandmother. This method of naming was especially popular with Sephardic Jews.

The French adopted the term fitz to mean son of: Fitzpatrick was therefore the son of Patrick (fitz was derived from the French work fils, which means son).

Spanish surnames are often derived from patronymics. In Spain and Portugal, an abbreviated way to identify a person with his or her father was by the addition of az, ez, iz, or oz to their father's last name. For instance, Julio, el hijo de Rodrigo became Julio Rodriquez (Julio, the son of Rodrigo).

And let's not forget that the Russians also used patronymics. It was common for Russians to have as their middle name the name of their father, with a *–vitch* added for the sons or *–evna or -ovna* added for their daughters. If I may borrow from author Leo Tolstoy's epic novel *Anna Karenina*, I will give you a few examples to illustrate this. The main character in the novel is Anna Arkadyevna Karenina – Anna, the daughter of Arkady. Her brother is Stepan Arkadyevich Oblonsky – Stepan, the son of Arkady. Konstantin Dmitrievitch Levin (Konstantin, son of Dmitri) was enamored with Anna's sister-in-law: Katarina Alexandrovna Oblonsky (Katarina, daughter of Alexandr), and Anna's lover was Alexey Kirillovitch Vronsky (Alexey, the son of Kirill), much to the dismay of her husband, Alexey Alexandrovitch Karenin (Alexey, the son of Alexandr). Phew!

While that may seem overwhelming, your Russian ancestors' very names may well contain clues to their next generation by providing their father's name.

> ### DON'T DO IT!
>
> I can almost guarantee that at some time or other in your research you will run across information that you'll "know" just isn't right. The temptation will be to correct the information rather than just write down what you have found.
>
> **Don't do it!**
>
> Perhaps it's the first name of an ancestor. While you might be absolutely certain that your great-great grandmother's name is Theodora, if you find her listed in a US Census as "Dolly," that is the name you should record as you copy the data down. Or perhaps it's your last name that has been spelled creatively, or a date that's not quite correct. Resist the temptation to substitute the information that is different. Copy the record exactly as you find it so that you can have an accurate representation of what you found.

Occupations

I suppose like most Americans, throughout your lifetime you have known many individuals named Miller, Smith, Carpenter, Carver, Schneider, Guerrero and Escobedo. Each of these surnames may be indicative that an ancestor owned or worked at a mill (Miller), was a blacksmith (Smith), built things (Carpenter), was one who carved (Carver), earned his keep as a tailor (Schneider means tailor in German), a soldier (Guerrero means soldier or warrior in Spanish) or worked as a sweeper (Escobedo). How about names like Joiner (construction term), or Metzger (German for butcher). I've a friend whose mother's maiden name was Kirchebauer – German for church builder.

Geographic Locations

Don't overlook the possibility that your surname is derived from a town, country, or physical geographic attribute associated with an ancestor. I once had two roommates named Mike. We called one Mike Jersey because he was from New Jersey. The concept is the same. Let's say there were two Mikes who lived near the same village several hundred years ago, before surnames were common. One lived by a lake, and the other at the foot of a hill. They might have been called Mike Lake and Mike Hill, respectively. I had a friend named Duane Alleman once, and I'd be willing to bet at least one of his paternal ancestors was German (Alemán is the Spanish word for German) who lived someplace where Spanish was spoken. Or how many people are you acquainted with who have the surname French? I'd wager somewhere in their family tree is a French ancestor.

As you climb your family tree, it is fun to be aware of these things – it just adds another element to your detective work.

Mother's Maiden Names

Another fairly common naming custom (or at least not uncommon!), has been the use of the mother's maiden name by one or more of her sons. I was once doing research on one of my family lines, and I came across a fellow named Hartle Hart Sellers. I wondered if Hart might not be his mother's maiden name, and sure enough, after much research, I found that Hart was indeed her maiden name. Again, a genealogical clue right in the midst of your ancestor's name!

Don't Assume...

As you are doing your research, don't fall into the trap that I once fell into. When I was a relatively inexperienced genealogist, I was doing research in central Pennsylvania. I was scouring the 1880 US Census, and discovered that one of my ancestors had married a young woman by the name of Mahala. What an interesting – and unique! – name that was. To determine her maiden name, I decided to search the 1870 US Census, when she would have been 11 or 12 years old. I reasoned that if I could find an 11- or 12-year-old girl named Mahala in one of the families in that county, I would probably have found her maiden name, since Mahala was such an odd name. Sure enough, after just a little bit of searching, I found an 11-year-old Mahala listed with her family not far from my own family on the census. I happily penned her maiden name on my forms and went merrily on my way. It wasn't until years later when I was doing additional research in that same county that I discovered that contrary to my assumption, Mahala was a very common name in 1870 Pennsylvania! Further research into other records proved the fallacy of my earlier assumption about her maiden name. (Mahala, by the way, is a Hebrew name meaning *Tender* and is often found in Jewish families.)

Another example – my brother-in-law had a great-great uncle named Adam. Adam died as a little boy. The next son born to that same family was named Adam after his older brother. He also died. Finally, a third son was born to the same family, and he too was named Adam. This Adam lived, but as my brother-in-law did his research, he had to be careful to get the right birthdate for the right Adam! (Note: Through the years, I have come to learn this was a fairly common practice.)

Spelling Woes

Here's a hint that is probably heresy to my sixth-grade teacher: Don't limit yourself to only one spelling of your name. In my research, in nearly every one of my family lines, at one time or another I have found variations in the spelling – sometimes within the same generation! Here are a few examples from my own family:

- Sellers, Sellars, Sellar

- Ritchie, Ritchey, Richey
- Horney, Harney
- Quillan, Quillen, Quillon, Quillin, McQuillan, McQuillon, etc.
- Lowrance/Lorentz
- McCollough/McCullough
- Rogers/Rodgers
- Throckmorton, Throgmorton
- Hudson/Hutson
- Graham/Grimes

And just because you are a Smith or a Jones (by the way - is it true that the surname of Adam and Eve was Jones?), don't assume you are immune from spelling changes: Smith/Smythe/Smithy/Schmidt or Jones/ Jonas/ Joans, etc.

There are many reasons for this, and your creative detective work will have to gather all the threads together into one cohesive answer. Immigration officials are often accused of this, but in my opinion that happened far less than was alleged. It may have been an immigration official, or it may have been years of family illiteracy or indifference. The spelling of my surname may be an example of the latter. The family tradition is that several generations of my farming ancestors saw no use in sending their children to school (or there wasn't one close enough to send them to). When the first kids in 75 years went to the local one-room schoolhouse, the teacher asked how they spelled their last name (the correct spelling was Quillan). The children responded that they didn't know, so the teacher "taught" them how to spell it: Quillen. No one at home knew better, so that spelling is the one my line of the family uses today. True story or false? I don't know, but I have seen family members' names spelled differently on US censuses, marriage licenses, birth certificates, and so on.

Another reason might be that a newly immigrated family wanted to fit in to their newly adopted country. In that case, Meier became Meyer, Schneider became Snider, Schmidt became Smith and Blau became Blue. In my family, McQuillan became Quillan.

What's in a Name? Checklist

____Write down all the possible spellings you can think of for the surname you are researching.

____Don't ignore surnames that are similar to but spelled differently than the one you are researching.

____Look for clues in your name that might indicate where an ancestor was born, or might indicate a possible occupational clue.

____Watch for patronymics and learn how to use them to help you in your ancestral search.

____If you come across a name that is spelled differently than how you think it should be spelled, write it down exactly as it appears in the research record.

____Because a name sounds strange or odd to your 21st-century ears, that doesn't mean it wasn't very common in the era or area where you are researching.

____Watch for middle names that might give a clue to a mother's maiden name.

Additional Resources

Rose, Christine, *Nicknames: Past and Present*, CR Publications, 2nd edition. (2007)

6

Census Records

About now, you may be wondering why there is a picture of a radish following this paragraph. It's because I think radishes are a gardener's best friend. No matter what you do, if you plant radishes, they will grow. Census Records remind me of radishes – whenever I use them, I almost always come away with genealogical information about my ancestors. They make me feel good, and I am making progress locating my ancestors. And the same will happen for you!

Who, What, When, Where, Why & How...

Perhaps you remember from your junior high or high school days the "5 Ws" of good journalism: telling the Who, What, When, Where, Why, and How of a given situation. That is exactly what the US Census does. The Constitution of the United States called for the enumeration (census) of all of its citizens beginning in 1790 and continuing every ten years after that. The earliest censuses were little more than tally marks of the population, gathered together under the head of a family. But as the years progressed, they evolved to the point that they gathered detailed information about each family and each family member in the United States.

Following is how censuses addressed the 5 Ws:

Who. Censuses were concerned with finding out the names of every person who lived in a certain area at a certain time. The censuses between 1790 and 1840 listed heads of family only, with tallies of all other persons in the household by age and sex. Every census since then has included the names and ages of each person living at that location.

What. The earliest US censuses focused on counting people only. As time went by, Congress realized their census enumerators could glean enormous amounts of detailed information about the population by asking just a few additional questions. From its beginnings as a tallying system, it grew to provide much more information (you'll see the questions asked during each census later in this chapter).

I like censuses because they often tell me more about the individuals than just their names (things like their birthplace, occupation, infirmities, etc.). It also gathers the individuals together into families.

When. In America, censuses were conducted in the first year of every decade. Each census was enumerated for a given date. For example, the

1910 census captured information about every individual who was living in a particular household as of April 15, 1910.

Due to privacy laws, the latest census available for the public to view is the 1950 census. (By law, individual records cannot be released to the public until 72 years after the census in which they were collected.) All censuses between 1790 and 1950 are available to view and search, except the 1890 census — almost all of it was lost in a tragic fire.

Where. Each census is very specific about where the people lived. The earliest censuses included the county and/or city where the family lived; later censuses included that information as well as the street addresses of the individuals.

Why. The initial reason for censuses was to determine legislative representation and for tax purposes. But Congress soon realized important demographic information could be compiled from the census. Hence questions about national origin, literacy and occupation gave them a snapshot of what the nation looked like.

How. Enumerators went from house to house carrying large binders or tablets with the census template, and spoke with whoever was home who could provide the information they were seeking. (Thank you from the bottom of my heart, enumerators!)

Questions, Questions, Questions

As time went on, the census forms evolved, and additional questions that were of interest to the government were added. Following are the various questions that were asked for each census:

1790
- Head of family
- Free White Males
- 16 and up, including head of family
- Under 16
- Free white females
- Including head
- All other persons
- Slaves
- County
- City

Note: No schedules are known to exist for the 1790 Census for Delaware, Georgia, Kentucky, New Jersey, Tennessee, and Virginia. It is thought that they were destroyed during the War of 1812 when the British attacked Washington. Some Virginia records are available from state enumeration records taken in 1790.

1800
- Head of family
- Free white males — Under 10, 10 to 16, 16 to 18, 16 to 26, 26 to 45, 45 and over
- Free white females — Under 10, 10 to 16, 16 to 18, 16 to 26, 26 to 45, 45 and over
- All others
- Slaves
- Remarks

1810

(Same as 1800)

1820
- Head of family
- Free white males — Under 10, 10 to 16, 16 to 18, 16 to 26, 26 to 45, 45 and over
- Free white females — Under 10, 10 to 16, 16 to 18, 16 to 26, 26 to 45, 45 and over
- Foreigners not naturalized
- Agriculture
- Commerce
- Manufacturers
- Free coloreds
- Slaves
- Remarks

1830
- Head of family
- Free white males
- Under 5, 5 to 10, 10 to 15, 15 to 20, 20 to 30, 30 to 40, 40 to 50, 50 to 60, 60 to 70, 70 to 80, 80 to 90, 90 to 100, over 100
- Free white females
- Under 5, 5 to 10, 10 to 15, 15 to 20, 20 to 30, 30 to 40, 40 to 50, 50 to 60, 60 to 70, 70 to 80, 80 to 90, 90 to 100, over 100
- Slaves
- Free colored

1840
(Same as 1830)

1850
- Name
- Age

- Sex
- Color
- Occupation
- Value of real estate
- Birthplace
- Married within year
- School within year
- Cannot read or write
- Enumeration date
- Remarks

1860
- Name
- Age
- Sex
- Color
- Occupation
- Value of real estate
- Value of personal property
- Birthplace
- Married in year
- School in year
- Cannot read or write
- Enumeration date
- Remarks

1870
- Name
- Age
- Sex
- Color

- Occupation
- Value of real estate
- Value of personal property
- Birthplace
- Father foreign born
- Mother foreign born
- Month born in census year
- School in census year
- Can't read or write
- Eligible to vote
- Date of enumeration

1880
- Name
- Color
- Sex
- Age June 1 in census year
- Relationship to head of house
- Single, Married, Widowed, Divorced
- Married in census year
- Occupation
- Other information
- Can't read or write
- Place of birth
- Place of birth of father
- Place of birth of mother
- Enumeration date

1890

Note: the vast majority of the 1890 census was destroyed in a tragic fire. Only fragments remain.

1900
- Name of each person whose place of abode on June 1, 1900 was in this family
- Relation to head of family
- Sex
- Color
- Month of birth
- Year of birth
- Age
- Marital status
- Number of years married
- Mother of how many children**
- Number of these children living**
- Place of birth
- Place of birth of father
- Place of birth of mother
- Years of immigration to US
- Number of years in US
- Naturalization
- Occupation
- Number of months not employed
- Attended school (months)
- Can read
- Can write
- Can speak English
- Home owned or rented
- Home owned free or mortgaged
- Farm or house

Note: the two questions marked by ** — although these questions may seem a little harsh, they have helped me find and gather to their family countless children who were born between the 1880 census and the 1900 census (remember – the 1890 census was destroyed). These questions flagged me to look for these children, who were born and died sometime during that twenty-year dark census period.

1910
  ·Name of each person whose place of abode on April 15, 1910 was in this family
   ·Relation to head of family
   ·Sex
   ·Race
   ·Age
   ·Marital status
   ·Number of years married
   ·Mother of how many children
   ·Number of these children living
   ·Place of birth
   ·Place of birth of father
   ·Place of birth of mother
   ·Years of immigration to US
   ·Naturalized or alien
   ·Language spoken
   ·Occupation
   ·Nature of trade
   ·Employer, worker or own account
   ·Number of months not employed
   ·Can read and write
   ·Attending school
   ·Home owned or rented
   ·Home owned free or mortgaged
   ·Farm or house

- Civil War veteran
- Blind or deaf-mute

1920
- Name of each person whose place of abode on January 1, 1920 was in this family
  - Relation to head of family
  - Home owned or rented
  - Home owned free or mortgaged
  - Sex
  - Color or race
  - Age
  - Marital status
  - Years of immigration to US
  - Naturalized or alien
  - Year of naturalization
  - Attending school
  - Can read or write
  - Place of birth
  - Mother tongue
  - Place of birth of father
  - Mother tongue of father
  - Place of birth of mother
  - Mother tongue of mother
  - Can speak English
  - Occupation

1930
- Name of each person whose place of abode on April 1, 1930 was in this family
  - Relationship of this person to the head of the family

- Home owned or rented
- Value of home, if owned, or monthly rental, if rented
- Radio set
- Does this family own a farm?
- Color or race
- Age at last birthday
- Marital condition
- Age at first marriage
- Attended school or college any time since Sept. 1, 1929
- Whether able to read or write
- Place of birth
- Place of birth of father
- Place of birth of mother
- Mother tongue (or native language) of foreign born
- Year of immigration into the United States
- Naturalization
- Whether able to speak English
- Trade, profession, or particular kind of work done
- Industry or business
- Class of worker
- Whether actually at work yesterday
- Whether a veteran of U.S. Military or naval forces
- What war or expedition
- Number of farm schedule

1940

- Street Address
- Name of each person whose place of abode on April 1, 1940 was in this family
- Relationship of this person to the head of the family
- Home owned or rented

- Is this a farm?
- Value of home, if owned, or monthly rental, if rented
- Color or race
- Sex
- Age at last birthday
- Marital Status
- Attended school of college since March 1?
- Highest grade of school attended
- Place of birth
- Citizenship of the foreign born?
- Residence on April 1, 1935
- Questions about hours / weeks worked during 1940
- Occupation / industry

1950
- Street Address
- Name of each person whose place of abode on April 1, 1950 was in this family
- Relationship of this person to the head of the family
- Home owned or rented
- Is this a farm?
- Value of home, if owned, or monthly rental, if rented
- Color or race
- Sex
- Age at last birthday
- Marital Status
- State or country of birth
- Attended school or college since March 1?
- Highest grade of school attended
- Place of birth
- Citizenship of the foreign born?

- Occupation / industry
- How much earned in 1949?
- Naturalization status if foreign born
- Occupation / industry
- A number of questions about work during the year
- If married, how many children had she given birth to?

After you've found your ancestor and his or her family on a census, what next? First and foremost, write down the information *exactly* as it appears on the census. As we discussed earlier in this chapter, writing the information down as it appears on the census is very important.

Tips and Tricks of the Census Trade

As wonderful as census records are, sometimes, for varying reasons, it's difficult to find your family members, even though you just know they had to have lived in the area you're searching. I have worked for years with censuses and have found a few tricks that allow me to find ancestors on the censuses even when they were playing very effective games of hide-and-go-seek. I will share these tricks over the course of the next few pages.

Check neighboring families

When you find your ancestor on a census, but they seem to disappear from subsequent censuses, look at the surrounding families for familiar surnames. Be sensitive to incorrect / different spellings of names. Knowing the maiden name of your ancestor may allow you to find others of her family nearby. Remember – several generations ago, families often stayed near one another for generations.

Let me give you an example:

My second great grandparents were William Huston Cunningham and

Amanda Stunkard Cunningham. I was fortunate to find them in the 1860 census of Wells Township, Fulton County, Pennsylvania:

Cunningham, William H. age 30
  Amanda age 26
  Sarah L. B. age 3
  Rachel age 1

One of the nice things about Amanda's maiden name — Stunkard – is that it's not a common name, and anyone nearby with that surname is bound to be related. Perhaps they are Amanda's parents, or brothers, uncles, cousins, etc. Searching nearby families, I find two families with the Stunkard surname:

Stunkard, William 52
  Margaret 50
  Robert F. 24
  Sara 21
  Eliza 19
  William 15

Stunkard, James M. 36
  Matilda 34
  Susan 11
  John 9

These two families are living in the same county and township as Amanda and William. The first couple, William and Margaret, could be Amanda's parents, as they are both the correct age to have a daughter Amanda's age (26 in 1860). Or perhaps they could be an aunt and uncle.

The other family – James M. and Matilda – could also be related to

Amanda. James is about the age where he could be an older brother of Amanda's. Or he could be a cousin. He's too old to be a son of William and Margaret.

Most of my family lived in rural America for most of their generations, especially the generations I would use censuses to find. Once I locate a member of my family in a county, I routinely search for other family members living nearby.

Check previous or subsequent censuses

Speaking of following threads, one way to do that is to check the census that was held ten years before, as well as ten years later, looking for clues that might tie up some loose ends. Using my previous example of 26-year-old Amanda Stunkard and checking ten years before in the 1850 census, I would look for a Stunkard family with a 16-year-old girl named Amanda. I'll also check for William and Margaret as well as James and Matilda. I'll check initially in the same county and state. Checking the 1850 census (remember – the 1850 census was the first to list the names of all family members), I find both those families:

Stunkard, William 42
   Margaret 40
   Robert F 14
   Sara 11
   Eliza 9

Stunkard, James M 26
   Matilda 24
   Susan 1
   Robert 24
   Amanda 16

I can use the children's names and ages to determine that these were the same families I found in the 1860 census. So – William and Margaret are in the same area ten years earlier, but the real find is 16-year-old Amanda living with James and Matilda, along with Robert. My assumption at this point is that James and Robert are Amanda's older brothers (because neither is old enough to be her father). Also, since other searches in the county, state and nation did not turn up Amanda's parents (Matthew and Sarah), I will assume they have died at this point.

While these are assumptions, I must still be open to the possibility that there are other reasons Amanda is living with James and Matilda. Perhaps she's a niece, or cousin. Perhaps her parents haven't died – maybe her parents really are William and Margaret – but she's merely moved in with James to help tend 1-year-old Susan because Matilda is ailing. Or...so many other possibilities. High on the possibility list, however, is that Amanda is living with her brother's family.

Be aware of places of birth

The 1880 census was the first to ask for the birth places of the parents as well as the individual. This is helpful as you try to match up families. For example, earlier I surmised that James M., Robert F. and Amanda Stunkard were siblings, since I found Robert F. and Amanda living with James M. If I can find these individuals in the 1880 census and see if they list their parents as being born in the same place, then I have one more piece of data tying them together.

Using these three potential siblings as an example, I search for them in the 1880 census. Without listing the rest of the family members, here's what I found for each:

James M. – no James M. He disappeared after the 1860 census...I surmise he has passed away.

Robert F. 54, born in Pennsylvania, father born in Pennsylvania, mother born in Pennsylvania

Amanda 46, born in Pennsylvania, father born in Pennsylvania, mother born in Pennsylvania

This information lends credence to my earlier assumption that Amanda and Robert F. may be siblings. James is probably a sibling as well, but that is a mystery that will have to be solved by additional research.

In my earlier example, I mentioned it might be possible that this couple William and Margaret could be the parents of 26-year-old Amanda. Even though the family Bible said Amanda's parents were Matthew and Margaret, I should still be open to the possibility that the father's name was William and not Matthew, or perhaps it was William Matthew and he went by William. But I also happen to know (from our family Bible) that some of Amanda's siblings are James McClelland, John, Robert Furgeson and Margaret. Several of William and Margaret Stunkard's children possibly shared those names (James M. and Robert F.), so I may be on the right track in thinking Amanda is living with her elder brothers. I think I need to do more research on this family! So many possibilities.

Be aware of other names listed with families

As you research the censuses, be aware of other individuals listed with your family, as they may provide you clues about your ancestors. For example, the 1900 census of Philadelphia, Pennsylvania lists this family:

Marley, Peter 35 Head
　Mary 32 Wife
Devlin, Elizabeth 70 Mother-in-law

If I were doing research on the Marley family and ran across this entry, I will have been fortunate enough to find Mary's maiden name. (Probably! Her mother could have remarried after Mary's father died.) Her mother,

Elizabeth Devlin, is living with her daughter. She was born in Ireland, and Mary was born in Pennsylvania. The record also tells me that Elizabeth immigrated to the United States in 1858. All of that is great information for me. And — as you'll learn in the *Immigration and Naturalization* chapter, I may be able to find information about Elizabeth and other members of her family if I can find their immigration and/or naturalization records.

Use all family members

This has been an especially successful tactic for me to use when an entire family drops out of sight between censuses. It works whether you are checking a previous census, or a subsequent census. It has been particularly effective in finding families where the names have been misspelled. A few years ago, I used this tactic to find my third and fourth great grandparents in the census. In both cases, their surnames had been misspelled, so that when I searched for the families in indexes, they did not appear. Instead of searching for a Quillen family, I instead searched the census in the county I thought the family was living in, using only the first name of my second great grandfather, Jonathan Quillen. When I did that, I found two families I had been unable to find for years! I went to the 1860 census for Lee County, Virginia, and searched for Jonathan; here's what I found:

Qulline, Frank 30
  Susannah 30
  Johnathan 12
  Martin 10

And as a bonus, living next door were my fourth great grandparents:

Quilling, Leven 70

Sillas 66
Henry 18
Salina 17
Ruthy 16
Savina 21

Note that the surnames for both families were misspelled – Qulline and Quilling and so they never came up when I searched indexes. Even though they misspelled Jonathan (Johnathan) on the census, it was close enough to come up as a hit. This is an especially effective tactic if one of the members of the family has an odd / peculiar / distinctive name. My family tree has an abundance of unique-ish names: Elzie, Versie, Alma, Estelle, Homer, Furgeson, Leonidas, Adelia, etc. I've had success using those names to search censuses when the surname had been misspelled or mis-transcribed in an index.

Use wildcards....

When you are searching indexes for your ancestors, some of the services (Ancestry.com, Footnote.com and FamilySearch.org) allow you to use wildcards in place of letters as you search for names. So, if I am having trouble finding an ancestor that I just know should be in the census (for example – the family is in the 1860 census and the 1880 census, but seemingly missing from the 1870 census), I might use wildcards in the spelling of their name. So instead of searching for Quillen, I can look for Qui***n. That covers Quillen, Quillan, Quillon, Quinlan, etc. This is an effective tool to use if an ancestor's name was misspelled in the census, or the indexer misinterpreted what was written on the census.

Advanced Search

Most of the subscription and free services you use to search census indexes allow you to do a brief search – surname, age and place of birth, for example. They all also offer advanced search capabilities, where you can really refine your request. This is especially nice if many people share your ancestor's surname (Smith, Jones, Johnson, etc.) in the area you area searching. Some of the options include:

First name
  Middle name
  Surname
  Place of birth
  Year of birth (+ or – 1, 2, 5, 10 and even 20 years)
  Place of residence
  Family members names (spouse, child, parents, siblings)

These advanced searches can narrow down the results of your search tremendously. But a caution: if you narrow your search too much, you may eliminate your ancestor because of poor information, misspellings, estimated birth dates that were wrong, etc. So if you use the advanced search capability and don't find your ancestor, don't worry. Just step back a bit and use fewer criteria.

Use the neighbors

This is a tactic I have used to find a number of my ancestors who had just "disappeared" from the censuses. When they disappear, try using a neighbor. Here's how: In the census where you found your ancestor, pick a neighboring family. See if you can find that family in the previous or subsequent censuses. If you find the neighbor, look around on the census pages before, on, and after the census page the neighbor is listed on to see if your family is nearby. Often, you'll find the family you're looking for, and their name is either unreadable, or was transcribed incorrectly so it didn't show up on and index.

Finding the Censuses

Thank goodness the Internet is the Information Powerhouse it now is. It will save you much time (and probably expense) over how you used to have to access censuses. Prior to the Internet, you needed to travel to one of fifteen regional centers located across the US to view microfilm copies of the censuses. Or you could order census records on microfilm from the LDS Church in Salt Lake City and have it shipped to a Family History Center near you to view. But that is no longer necessary. Within minutes of sitting down at your computer, you can access census records in the US and many other countries in the world. Thank you, Ancestry.com and FamilySearch.org. These two giants of genealogical research paved the way for easy access to census records. Both provide access to all censuses that are now available.

I heartily recommend using census records to begin finding your ancestors – because unless your ancestors were uncannily wary, you stand a great chance of finding them on one or many censuses.

So – let me share one more example that is close to home for me. The latest US census available is the 1950 census. My grandparents were living in Norman, Oklahoma during the census. My father, William E. Quillen, was 19 years old in 1950. Let's see if we can find them in the 1950 census.

Since you're just beginning in genealogy, you probably don't have an Ancestry.com account, nor a FamilySearch.org account. Since the latter is free, let's do your research using FamilySearch.org. I'll carry that through most of the rest of the book – I'll show you how to do things in FamilySearch because you can go try it yourself immediately without having to pay for a subscription. The time may come that you'll decide to pay for a subscription, but for our purpose – helping you get started doing genealogy – we'll use FamilySearch. About half the genealogists I know use FamilySearch as their principal genealogy search tool, and the other half uses Ancestry. You might try a trial subscription with

Ancestry (as of this writing, they offer a free two-week trial) to see if you like it enough to shell out the subscription fee – or not!

Back to our task at hand — go to FamilySearch.org. If you've not already done so, set up a new account with them. It's pretty intuitive, so you shouldn't have any problems.

Once you are registered with them, login and go to the FamilySearch.org home page. At the top, you'll see a list of options – click on *Search*. In the drop-down box, click on *Records*. On the right-hand side of the page you're sent to, you'll see the opportunity to enter a person's first and last names, the place you think they were living in 1950, and their birth year. Use my father's information to fill in the box: William E. Quillen, Norman, Oklahoma, 1930. Once you've entered the information, click on *Search*.

You'll be taken to a page that lists a few men named William E. Quillen... select the one whose parents are Helon and Vivian Quillen (it was the first choice in the list for me, but may not be for you). Click on William's name, and you'll be taken to a transcription of his entry; on the left is an image of the actual census page. Click on the image, and then enlarge it (by clicking the + sign several times) and scroll down until you find my father and his folks. You'll see:

CENSUS RECORDS

It won't look exactly like that – my father and his folks are in the middle of the census page, but I wanted you to see the column headings, so I cut-and-pasted them together.

The information you can glean here for my young father includes: his name, relation to the head of the house, his race, sex and age. The next column asks if he is married, and the response, though a little difficult to see, is Nev – Never. His parents' designation is Mar – married. And all three were born in Oklahoma.

See? Piece o' cake! Now – try this with someone you know and see how it works for you! The best way for you to learn how to use the censuses...is to use them. Again and again.

And now you have made your first venture into the world of Genealogy. As fun as this has been, it only gets better after this!

Other Census Records

There are a number of other census records that may be of value to you.

Slave Schedules

When I first learned about slave schedules, I got very excited, thinking these would be a welcome tool for genealogists doing research on African Americans. Alas, the slave schedules turned out to be nothing more than tally marks categorizing slaves as male, female and their ages, much akin to the US censuses prior to 1840.

In addition to age, gender and race, the slave schedules asked whether or not the slave had been manumitted (freed / emancipated) or whether the slave was a fugitive from the state. It also asked for the number of slave houses in existence.

Separate slave schedules were enumerated during the 1850 and 1860 censuses. Prior to that, they were included in the tally of the slave owner's family. The 1840 census for Henry Clay of Bourbon County, Kentucky shows a family of three adults (one apparently his mother or mother-in-law), four children and 47 slaves of varying ages and sexes.

In the 1850 and 1860 slave schedules, slaves are listed under the slave owner's name, but a notation indicates whether they were in the employ of another individual. But still, these listings provide only the slave owner's name and the name of the individual who rented the slave from the owner.

(A terrible time in our nation's history!)

CENSUS RECORDS

United States 1860 slave schedule for the Eastern District, Bourbon County, Kentucky for Henry Clay:

Age	Gender	Race
87	Female	Black
71	Male	Black
65	Male	Black
60	Female	Black
46	Female	Black
45	Male	Black
36	Male	Black
31	Male	Black
30	Male	Mulatto
30	Female	Black
28	Male	Mulatto

In addition to age, gender and race, the slave schedules asked whether or not the slave had been manumitted (freed / emancipated) or whether the slave was a fugitive from the state. It also asked for the number of slave houses in existence.

Mortality Schedules

Another important census schedule that was kept coincident with the US Census was the Mortality Schedule for the 1850 through 1880 censuses. These schedules listed everyone who had died between June 1 of the year before the census and May 31 of the census year. They list the name, age, sex, marital status, race, occupation, birthplace, cause of death and length of illness for each individual who passed away during that year. If you have an opportunity to search Mortality Schedules, you may find it interesting to note the ages of those who died. So many of them are children under age 10 - infant and young child mortality was very high in the mid-1800s. I guarantee it will tug at your heartstrings. Here is a sample from the 1860 Mortality Schedules for Chester county, Pennsylvania:

Name	Age	Sex	Place of Birth	Month Died
Hannah McCoy	10/12	F	Penn	March
Martha A Harry	14	F	Penn	October
Sarah Mace	1	F	Penn	April
Morrison Mace	10	M	Penn	September

These children didn't make it to the June 1 cut-off for the 1860 census. To be considered for this census schedule, they would have had to have died between June 1, 1859 and May 31, 1860. These little / young ones in the record above died in March 1860, October 1859, April 1860 and September 1859. Columns to the right of these listed their affliction and length of time they'd had it. (Note Sarah and Morrison were probably siblings who died eight months apart.)

Census Records Checklist

____Find the location of the nearest facility that has US Census records, or select a genealogy website you want to use, such as FamilySearch.org, Ancestry.com, Fold3.com, etc.

____Determine which surnames you want to search for.

____Determine the name of the head of household if not the ancestor you are looking for.

____Know the approximate birth year of the ancestors you are searching for.

____Try and discover the family's place of residence during the census year

____If possible, identify the names of siblings and parents of the ancestors you are searching for (this will help you identify the correct family).

____ Mortality schedules will tell you all individuals who died between June 1 in the year previous to the census, through May 31 of the census year. They're a good source to find the very young and the very old.

Additional Resources

Quillen, W. Daniel, *Mastering Census and Military Records*, Cold Spring Press, (2014)

Carlberg, Nancy Ellen, *Beginning Census Research*, Carlberg Press (2009)

Dollarhide, William, *The Census Book: A Genealogist's Guide to Federal Census Facts, Schedules and Indexes*, Heritage Quest (1999)

7

Military Records

America has fought many military conflicts and wars throughout her history. The military likes to keep track of their men, and many of those records hold important genealogical information that genealogists love to find.

American Wars

If you are not sure whether one of your ancestors fought in one of America's wars, see if they were of military age (roughly ages 16 to 35) during any of these wars:

- French and Indian Wars (1754 to 1763)
    - Revolutionary War (1775 to 1783)
    - War of 1812 (1812 to 1815)
    - Mexican-American War (1846 to 1848)
    - Civil War (1861 to 1865)
    - Spanish-American War (1898)
    - Philippine War (1899 to 1902)
    - World War I (1917 to 1918)
    - World War II (1941 to 1945)

MILITARY RECORDS

- Korean Conflict (1950 to 1953)
- Vietnam War (1965 to 1973)

If any of your male ancestors were of military age during any of those wars, it may well be worth your time to check out military records for genealogical information.

Where to Begin?

To begin, look at the list of American wars above. If you have an ancestor that would have been of military age during that war, there is a possibility there are military records for him.

Let's use my third great grandfather as an example. Leonidas Horney was born in 1817. That would have made him the ripe old age of 44 at the time the Civil War broke out in 1861. Was he too old to participate in the Civil War? Perhaps. But it also put him at about the age of senior military officers. So, I might as well check Civil War military records to see if he may have served. Another possibility is that he may have served during the Mexican-American War when he was a young man. So I should check those records also.

In Leonidas' case, I had a bit of a clue, in that I have a picture of him in a Union Civil War uniform.

I decided to begin with a great (and free) website for locating soldiers (and sailors). It is owned by the National Parks Service at *www.nps.gov/civilwar*. After going to that website, I clicked on *People*, and then in the drop-down box, I selected *Soldiers and Sailors Database*. I selected *Soldiers* in the next drop-down box, and was provided with a place to enter my third great grandfather's name. When I did so and hit Return, I received this information about him:

Horney, Leonidas

BATTLE UNIT NAME: 10th Regiment, Missouri Infantry
　SIDE: Union
　COMPANY: A
　SOLDIER'S RANK IN: Captain
　SOLDIER'S RANK OUT: Lieutenant Colonel

The *Soldiers and Sailors Database* still has its records on microfilm, and I could have gone through a bit of a complicated process to order copies of the information. Instead, I decided jump over to Fold3.com (a subscription service that is part of the Ancestry.com family specializing in military records) to see what else I could find for him.

I hit the jackpot! The first thing I found was his *Compiled Military Service Record* which showed his enlistment, his progress from Captain to Lieutenant Colonel, and finally, the last sad line read:

May 1863 Killed in action at the Battle of Champion Hills, 16 May 1863.

I also found his wife's application for a pension as a result of Leonidas's death. There were eight or ten pages; here is the page listing her children who were under age 16 at the time of their father's death (a requirement to be considered for a pension that included monies to support the children under age 16):

[Handwritten letter to the Commissioner of the Pension Office listing children under sixteen years of age: William Jeffery Thorney born March 14, 1849, aged 14; Mary Jane Thorney born June 30, 1851, aged 12; Emilia Ann Thorney born July 16, 1857, aged 5; Adele Thorney born August 27, 1860, aged 2. Signed Jane Thorney, January 27, 1864, Schuyler County, Illinois.]

The children were ages 14, 12, 5 and 2. What a toll the Civil War took on families!

    Several other pages included information about their marriage date and place, which had been certified by the county clerk of their home county.

    Leonidas's wife must have dotted all the I's and crossed all the T's correctly – she was granted a pension of $30 per month for the rest of her life (or until she remarried). She never did remarry, and died 44 years later, in 1907.

You can see now why I get so excited about military records as a great source of genealogical information!

The National Archives

At some point in your search for the military records of your ancestors, you will probably cross paths with the National Archives of the United States of America. The repository of all US military records, the National Archives will likely yield you a great deal of genealogical information, if you only know (or learn) how to use them. Unfortunately, most of their records are still on microfilm, but several genealogical companies have been granted permission to make digital copies of those records. That work is still ongoing.

Here are the types of records available:

Enlistment Records

Enlistment records for soldiers do not generally contain much genealogical information. Typically, they will tell you the name, rank, date and place that the individual enlisted. They may also tell you such interesting tidbits as their occupation, age, physical description (height, weight, hair and eye color, complexion, size of hands and feet, etc.) and marital status.

Compiled Military Service Records (CMSR)

Every volunteer soldier has a Compiled Military Service Record (CMSR) for each regiment he served in. It contains basic information about his service career while in that regiment. Information contained within the record might be enlistment information, leave (vacation) requests, muster (roll call) records, and injury or illness reports. If he was killed in action, this will most likely be found in the CMSR.

When I found the service record for Colonel Leonidas Horney, my third great grandfather, I received documents that included the following:

·The date and place of his enlistment;
  ·His date of birth;
  ·His height, hair and eye color and color of complexion;
  ·The rank he enlisted as;
  ·The commanders he reported to;
  ·Several documents detailing his promotion from Captain to Major to Lieutenant Colonel;

Two casualty sheets, one detailing an minor injury early in the War, and the other reporting his death at Champion Hill, Mississippi on May 16, 1863.

> **Poignant Discovery**
>
> I knew my third great grandfather had served as a colonel in the Civil War under Ulysses S. Grant, and I also knew that he was killed in a skirmish just prior to the Siege of Vicksburg. But I was unprepared for the article I found in his hometown newspaper:
>
> *Colonel Horney Killed!*
>
> "*A private letter written to a gentleman in St. Louis, Missouri from Vicksburg under the date May 20th, and published in Monday morning's Democrat, gives the sad news that Colonel Leonidas Horney, of the 10th Missouri Regiment, was killed before Vicksburg. This is indeed bitter news to his family and many friends in this county. Let us hope the intelligence may not be confirmed.*"
>
> Unfortunately, the intelligence was confirmed. The death of this small-town war hero was an important and tragic event in the history of this village.

Pensions

As you've read, military pension applications can be a rich source of genealogy information on your ancestors. Military pensions were applied for by Union army soldiers, their widows and / or their minor children. Because of the need to ensure the applicant was indeed related to the former soldier, a great deal of information was often requested to substantiate the relationship. A widow, for example, would have had to provide the date and place of their marriage (and often the name of the person who performed the marriage). She would often be required to provide either the marriage certificate, or a certified record signed by the minister who performed the ceremony, or the county clerk of the county they were married in. If the widow had children under the age of 16, she also needed to provide proof of their birth in the form of a birth certificate, or a government-certified document that provided the child's name, birth date and birth place – all genealogical nuggets.

Pension files are all indexed by the **National Archives and Records Administration** (NARA), and the index is available at National Archives locations or at the following website: *www.archives.gov/research_room/ genealogy/*
 military/pension_index_1861_to_1934.html.

Ancestry.com, Fold3.com and FamilySearch.org all have large military record collections, including many pensions, and many of them are online. I've found Fold3 to be the best of the bunch for military records. (Note – if you're looking to go to the National Archives, note that there is another subscription service named Archives.com. The National Archives website is *www.archives.**gov**.*)

Confederate Records

A special note about Confederate army records. Both Compiled Military Service Records (CMSR) and Records of Events were kept for Confederate units. They are often not as complete as Union records of the same type, as many Confederate records did not survive the war. Pensions were granted to Confederate veterans and their widows and minor children by the states of Alabama, Arkansas, Florida, Georgia, Kentucky, Louisiana, Mississippi, Missouri, North Carolina, Oklahoma, South Carolina, Tennessee, Texas, and Virginia. Note that it was the *states* who granted these pensions, not the federal government; those records are contained in the State Archives of the state where the veteran resided after the war, not in the National Archives.

Draft Registration Cards

Another marvelous set of American military records are **Draft Registration Cards**. When the United States joined World War I in 1917, the Federal government required all men ages 18 to 45 to register for the draft. Even non-citizens living in the United States were required to register! (Experts estimate that 98% of the men living in America in 1917 registered for the draft.) While the information is somewhat brief, it can provide secondary resource information about such things as a young man's birth date and place, his mother's, father's, or wife's name.

So – if you have a male ancestor that was born between 1877 and 1897, there is a 98% chance he had a World War I draft registration card out there somewhere – just waiting to be found.

When World War II broke out, the US government required all men who were born between 1877 and 1897 to register for the draft. It was called the *Old Men's Draft*. That range of years covered my great grandfather's birth, and he registered. Here's an image of his World War II draft registration card:

MILITARY RECORDS

```
REGISTRATION CARD—(Men born on or after April 28, 1877 and on or before February 16, 1897)
SERIAL NUMBER    1. NAME (Print)                                              ORDER NUMBER
U  1566          Edgar          Estelle         Quillen
                      (First)          (Middle)        (Last)
2. PLACE OF RESIDENCE (Print)
                          Ralston              Pawnee    Okla.
      (Number and street)    (Town, township, village, or city)  (County)   (State)
    [THE PLACE OF RESIDENCE GIVEN ON THE LINE ABOVE WILL DETERMINE LOCAL BOARD
    JURISDICTION; LINE 2 OF REGISTRATION CERTIFICATE WILL BE IDENTICAL]
3. MAILING ADDRESS
        Ralston, Oklahoma.
           [Mailing address if other than place indicated on line 2.  If same insert word same]
4. TELEPHONE                   5. AGE IN YEARS          6. PLACE OF BIRTH
        X                           61                  Cumberland Gap
                                   DATE OF BIRTH                (Town or county)
        X                      Jan.  15   1881         West Virginia
    (Exchange)  (Number)       (Mo.)  (Day)  (Yr.)           (State or country)
7. NAME AND ADDRESS OF PERSON WHO WILL ALWAYS KNOW YOUR ADDRESS
            Dolly Quillen(Wife)  Ralston, Oklahoma
8. EMPLOYER'S NAME AND ADDRESS
            Self
9. PLACE OF EMPLOYMENT OR BUSINESS
            Farming near Ralston, Oklahoma.
     (Number and street or R.F.D. number)           (Town)        (County)      (State)
     I AFFIRM THAT I HAVE VERIFIED ABOVE ANSWERS AND THAT THEY ARE TRUE.
D. S. S. Form 1                  16—21630-1          Ed Quillen
 (Revised 4-1-42)     (over)                            (Registrant's signature)
```

Note the genealogy information we discover on this record – his birth date and place, and his wife's name. (Although her legal name was Theodora Charity – but they called her Dolly!)

In case you're wondering, America was not planning to draft these men who were between 44 and 64 years of age – they were trying to determine what skills might be available if all the young men in America were called up to go fight.

I have used draft registration cards in my genealogical research time and time again, and the information I gleaned from them allowed me to find primary-source vital records for many of my ancestors. They have also allowed me to get past genealogical brick walls that I was experiencing. Perhaps they will do that for you too!

These records can all be found at the National Archives, Ancestry.com, FamilySearch.org, MyHeritage.com, and Fold3.com.

Military Records Checklist

____Identify an ancestor you think may have served in the military.

____Decide what you want to learn.

____Understand what military records are available to research.

____Understand the process for obtaining records (Internet, mail request, personal visit).

Additional Resources

Quillen, W. Daniel, *Mastering Census and Military Records*, Cold Spring Press, (2014)

Beers, Henry Putney, *The Confederacy: A Guide to the Archives of the Confederate States of America*, Smithsonian Institution Press, (August 1986)

General Index to Pension Files 1861–1934, National Archives and Records Administration Microfilm Publication T288. (www.archives.gov/research/military/pension-genealogy/1861-1934.html)

Hewett, Janet B., editor, *The Roster of Union Soldiers, 1861 – 1865*, 33 volumes. Wilmington, North Carolina, Broadfoot Publishing, 1997.

Johnson, Richard S., *How to Locate Anyone Who is or Has Been in the Military*, 7th edition, Fort Sam Houston, Texas: Military Information Enterprises, 1999.

US War Department, *The War of Rebellion: A Compilation of the Official Records of the Union and Confederate Armies,* reprint: Gettysburg, Pennsylvania, The National Historical Society (2022)

8

Immigration and Naturalization Records

If your family is like mine, your ancestors include many who immigrated to America from other countries. Six of my eight great grandparents have Irish surnames, and five of those six lines came from Northern Ireland.

And good news – immigration and naturalization records (particularly the latter) are rich in genealogical information.

I used the general phrase *immigration and naturalization* records. These terms, although often used together, indicate two distinct types of information:

Immigration records

Immigration records refer to those records that detail information about your ancestors' trip (immigration) to America. The most valuable of these records include:

Ship passenger lists – these are the rosters of all who traveled on a particular ship to the United States. They are sometimes called **ship manifests**. These records, especially in later immigration years, contain a great deal of information of genealogical value.

Censuses – censuses might not seem like they would contain immigration or naturalization information, but some censuses do. The federal censuses for 1900 through 1950 (1940 and 1950 only asked one question each) each asks a series of questions that may provide clues that will assist you in finding these ocean-going (mountain-climbing, desert-crossing) ancestors of yours. By census, here are the immigration and naturalization questions asked:

1900
- If an immigrant, the year of immigration to the United States
- How long the immigrant has been in the United States
- Is the person naturalized?

1910
- Year of immigration to the United States
- Whether naturalized or alien
- Whether able to speak English, or, if not, give language spoken

1920
- Year of immigration to the United States
- Naturalized or alien
- If naturalized, year of naturalization

1930
- Year of immigration into the United States
- Naturalization
- Whether able to speak English

1940
- Citizenship of the foreign born

1950
  ·Naturalization status if foreign born

Naturalization records

Naturalization records refer to those records immigrants completed after arriving in America in order to become US citizens. There are several:

Declarations of Intent – these were documents completed to indicate the immigrant's intention to become a US citizen. They were often completed immediately upon arrival in the United States, but were sometimes completed years later. These are often called *first papers*. These documents usually have a great deal of genealogical information in them.

Petitions for Naturalization – these papers were completed by the immigrant as part of his or her formal request to become a US citizen. Generally speaking, these could not be completed until an immigrant had been in the US at least five years. Also called *second papers* or *final papers*, as well as *Petition for Citizenship*. These papers usually have a great deal of genealogical information in them.

Where are these records?

So how do we find these immigration and naturalization records / genealogical gold mines? Up to this point, I've used FamilySearch when I provided examples, so you didn't need a subscription service to try them yourself. But as I wrote this, many of FamilySearch's immigration and naturalization documents are not yet online, so we can either use Ancestry.com, Fold3.com (part of the Ancestry.com family), or we can use another free website for Ellis Island (where many Irish immigrants arrived).

Ellis Island

If your ancestors immigrated to America between 1892 and 1924, you'll definitely want to check out the Ellis Island website. Through the years it was active, over twelve million immigrants entered the country through Ellis Island's gates.

To be honest, as much as I really like the Ellis Island website and the genealogical information it can provide for me, I find navigating the website a bit...clunky. So let me walk you through an example.

Go to *heritage.statueofliberty.org*. You will be brought to this page:

PASSENGER SEARCH
Explore our vast database of 65 million passenger records...
? Need more information? Click here.

Let's see if an Irishman named Patrick McQuillan ever came through Ellis Island on his way to America (I selected the first name randomly – Patrick is a popular given name in Ireland). Enter his first and last names in the appropriate boxes, and then hit *Return*.

When I did this, I received a list of 19 men named Patrick McQuillan who had immigrated through Ellis Island. I selected the fourth one down, a Patrick McQuillan who came in 1923. Here's what his line looks like:

McQuillan, Patrick   1923   Clydebank, Scotland   Leviathan

I clicked on the icon on the far-right of the line, and was taken to a login page. I suspect you won't have an account yet, so at the bottom of the box, click *Create Account*. It is free, so take a minute or two to create an account. When your account creation is complete and you login, you'll receive information about Patrick:

McQuillan, Patrick

PASSENGER ID: 6000760080075
FRAME: 650
LINE NUMBER: 15
SHIP NAME: Leviathan
PORT OF DEPARTURE: Southampton
ARRIVAL DATE: November 3rd, 1923

You'll also receive a scare (I did!), because right below this, is the opportunity to purchase Patrick's passenger record for $29 or $49 (depending on what you want to order). Don't worry – you don't have to purchase the passenger list page to be able to view it. Just scroll down past the advertisement to the last quarter of the page, and you'll see one of Patrick's two passenger list pages. Click on the one listed, and it will take you to his location on the passenger list. Unfortunately, it's the *second* page of the list, so you'll need to go one page earlier. Patrick's page (650) will be shown on the right-hand side of the page, highlighted in yellow.

Click on the up arrow, and select the previous page / frame: 649. Then click the blue box that says *Full Image* to see a larger image of the page. Then you'll see the page where Patrick's name appears (he is on line 15).

As you read across his line, you can get to know this 15-year-old young man – it appears he's a member of a portion of a family traveling to the United States. His mother Elizabeth is two lines above him, and his brothers John and James are on the lines above and below him, (on his mother's line, we also learn he has at least one brother who is still in Scotland — Michael). His last residence was Clydebank, Scotland, and his family's destination is Brooklyn, New York. Now – go back to page 650 for the second half of Patrick's line to learn more about him.

Enlarge the page and go to lines 13 through 16, and then you'll learn that he and his mother and brothers are coming to America to be with their husband and father, Adam McQuillan, who lives in Brooklyn. We also learn that he and his brother James were born in Clydebank, Scotland and his mother and brother John were born in Glasgow, Scotland.

As you can see – there is a lot of great genealogy information available on Ellis Island passenger lists.

But what about their father Adam? Can we find any records for him? I checked the Ellis Island website, and discovered...nothing. So here's where your detective skills come into play. I pondered where he may have arrived in America, if not New York's Ellis Island? I knew that a lot of Irish arrived in Boston, just a hop, skip, and a jump from New York, so I again used Ancestry.com and looked there – and found an Adam McQuillan from Clydebank, Scotland, who had arrived in America two months earlier.

The passenger list I found contained a lot of important information about Adam McQuillan. It told me he was 53 years old, a machine man, born in Ireland, but most recently lived in Clydebank, Scotland. While many families preferred to travel together, others sent a member of the family – typically the father or an older son – ahead to find employment, find a place to live, make arrangements, etc. Early in my marriage, I moved my family from Utah to New Jersey (talk about a journey to a foreign country!). I went ahead of the family, scouted areas to live that were close enough to my place of work, and rented a home. I have seen this repeated many, many times among the immigrant families I have researched. So, if in your research you come across an immigrating family without a husband, don't be unduly alarmed or saddened.

The second page of the passenger list Adam was on provided more information about the McQuillan family. It tells us that Adam was born in Belfast, Ireland (Northern Ireland didn't become an entity until 1922), and it said the relative he was going to join in the United Sates was Ellen McQuillan, his daughter, who lived in Brooklyn, New York. So now, between Adam's and Elizabeth's Boston and New York passenger lists, we're beginning to get a picture of this Scottish / Irish family:

- Adam McQuillan, head of household, age 53
- Elizabeth McQuillan, wife, age 50

- William McQuillan, son, age ? (Elizabeth's nearest relative in Scotland – listed as her son)
- Ellen McQuillan, daughter, age ? (the relative Adam was going to join in the US)
- John McQuillan, son, age 17
- Patrick McQuillan, son, age 15
- James McQuillan, son, age 9

I decided to see if I could find Adam's **Declaration of Intent** (first papers) and / or his *Petition for Citizenship* (second papers). Using Ancestry.com, I was quickly able to find both. Here is his *Declaration of Intent*:

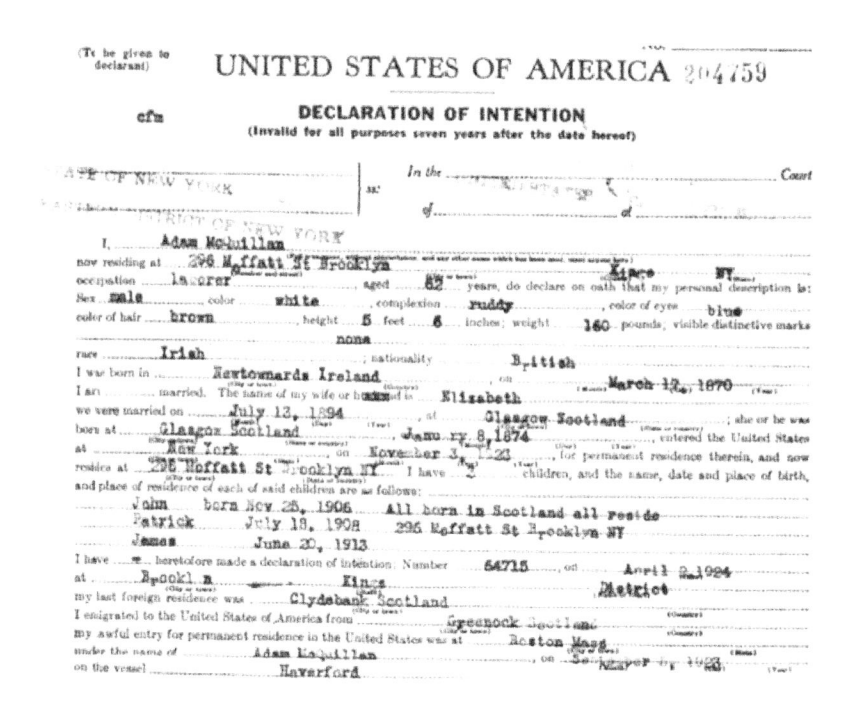

Wow — what a find! Adam's Declaration of Intent shows me:

- Adam's birth date and place (March 17, 1870 – St. Patrick's Day!)
- Adam's wife Elizabeth's birth date and place
- Their marriage date and place
- The birth dates and places for his three sons

Now – as wonderful as this is genealogically – it's not perfect. For example, from their respective ship passenger lists, we know that Adam and Elizabeth have at least two other children – Ellen (Brooklyn, NY) and Michael (Clydebank, Scotland). Also, there are minor discrepancies between Adam's Declaration of Intent and his Petition for Citizenship. A few dates are a day or two off (one of his son's birth dates), or a year or two off (his wife's age). But they're close – and will allow us perhaps to find more accurate information elsewhere.

As you can see, if you had ancestors who immigrated to America, these documents can help you discover more about them quickly.

Ports of Entry

Many individuals believe that all immigrants to the United States came through Ellis Island. But – even though there were 300 ports of entry into the US, the vast majority of immigrants came through a handful of ports. Below is a list of the busiest immigrant ports between 1820 and 1920, along with the estimated number of immigrants processed. Between 1820 and 1920, immigrants entered the US in the following numbers at the following points:

Baltimore, MD – 1,460,000
Boston, MA — 2,050,000
Charleston, SC – 20,000
Galveston, TX – 110,000
Key West, FL – 130,000
New Bedford, MA – 40,000

New York City, NY – 23,960,000 (Ellis Island and its predecessor Castle Garden)
New Orleans, LA – 710,000
Passamaquoddy, ME – 80,000
Philadelphia, PA – 1,240,000
Portland / Falmouth, ME – 120,000
Providence, RI – 40,000
San Francisco, CA – 500,000

Given those numbers, the top ports in order of arrival in the United States were:

New York
Boston
Baltimore
Philadelphia
New Orleans
San Francisco

Those ports accounted for the processing of nearly 30 million immigrants over that 100-year period. That's a peck and two-thirds of immigrants!

A couple of final things to keep in mind when searching for naturalization records – women did not need to file naturalization papers (although some did) – they could become citizens through their husband's naturalization process. Same with minor children – they could become citizens when their father became a citizen.

Immigration and Naturalization Checklist

_____Ship Passenger Lists (aka Ship Manifests) often held important genealogical information about the immigrants (particularly in later years!)

____The 1910 through 1950 censuses asked specific questions about immigration and naturalization status. Check 'em out!

____Ellis Island wasn't the only port / immigration location immigrants entered the United States through.

____Declarations of Intent and Petitions for Citizenship often provided important information about immigrants and their families.

____Understand where to find immigration and naturalization records.

____Women may or may not have naturalization paperwork – they could choose to be naturalized through their husband's naturalization process, or do it themselves. Most did it through their husbands' processes.

Additional Resources

Quillen, W. Daniel, *Mastering Immigration and Naturalization Records*, Cold Spring Press (2015)

9

Using the Church of Jesus Christ of Latter-day Saints

The Genealogical Society of Utah, affiliated with the Church of Jesus Christ of Latter-day Saints, is one of the premier genealogical organizations in the world. The Genealogical Society of Utah and the **LDS church** have been actively involved in collecting genealogical information for over 150 years. Working with foreign governments, they have been methodically and tirelessly microfilming countless governmental and church records throughout the world.

Even as you read this, hundreds of volunteers are scattered across the globe photographing records. At the time of this printing, records have been filmed in over 140 countries. The good news is that this information is then archived, and is available to anyone with a willingness to search through their records for them – whether they are members of the LDS church or not. There are three important areas you need to learn about as you become familiar with this wonderful resource for research. Those three areas are:

- FamilySearch™ Library
  - FamilySearch™ website
  - FamilySearch™- Centers

Let's talk about each one of these resources:

The FamilySearch Library

You may or may not have heard the term Family History Library. It is nerve central for all this genealogical activity is in Salt Lake City, Utah in a large building now known as the **FamilySearch Library**. The library was founded in 1894 with the intent of assisting members of the LDS church with their family history research. Since that time, the library and its resources have been made available to all, regardless of their religious affiliation. The building that currently houses the library is located at 35 North West Temple in Salt Lake City (Tel. 801/240-2331). It is open Monday from 9:00am to 6:00pm, Tuesday through Thursday from 9:00am to 8:00pm, and Friday and Saturday 10:00am to 6:00pm. It is closed on Sundays, January 1, July 4, Thanksgiving and December 24 and 25.

The genealogical collection is housed on five floors (four of them open to the public). At 142,000 square feet, it is the largest library of its kind in existence. Lighting, humidity and temperature control in the library are designed to protect the precious genealogical records from deterioration. And is it ever a busy place! Hundreds of volunteers and full- and part-time employees labor to assist an average of 2,000 visitors that come through its doors each day. There is no charge to enter the library or use its services, nor is there a need to call for reservations.

The library boasts a genealogical collection that makes the mouth of any genealogist water. There are over 340,000 books in the library's collections, most of them family histories. Their genealogical collection grows - mostly through the efforts of volunteers − exponentially annually. It is estimated that over 5.2 *billion* images – books, censuses, wills, etc., are available to research, and there are billions of names contained in these records. That's a lot of people, and many of your ancestors are likely to be contained in those records.

I have been to the FamilySearch Library, and it is as impressive as it sounds. For a time, I was fortunate enough to live in Salt Lake City, and I worked just a few blocks from the Library. Often, I would arrange to take my morning break at 11:45am, my lunch at noon and my afternoon break at 1:00pm, giving me nearly an hour and a half to do research on a fairly regular basis. Good idea, right? Wrong...I had to stop that practice because I found that I was continually calling back to the office and taking the afternoon off as vacation because I had found a lead I just had to follow up on. While my ancestors loved it, my wife was not too thrilled about the practice.

FamilySearch Library volunteers and employees (400 to 500 each day!) are excited to assist you in your research efforts whether you are just beginning your search, or whether you have been doing it for many years. They have experts in a variety of areas, including various foreign countries. They can help you get started or continue to unravel a genealogical mystery that you have been wrestling with for years.

I have had personal experiences of finding long-lost relatives while researching within the walls of this Library, and many friends can tell stories of searches with happy endings as a result of visits to the Family History Library.

Getting Around Salt Lake City

If you are fortunate enough to travel to Salt Lake City to visit and spend time in the Family History Library, you will likely be befuddled by seemingly incomprehensible addresses in Salt Lake City. You'll encounter addresses like:

709 North 700 East

2392 East 4400 South
1332 West 7100 South

Confusing, right? Wrong - once you understand the format, you will never need a map to get around in Salt Lake City. And the format is logical and easy: the first number and direction represent the street address; the second number and direction are the name of the street. There – got it? No? Read on.

The key to unfolding the mystery of these addresses is the LDS Temple in downtown Salt Lake City. All addresses in Salt Lake City tell you their relative location to the temple. For example, the address 4684 West 3100 South tells you that the house or building is located 46.84 blocks west of the temple and is on 3100 South Street (31 blocks south of the temple). Taking the addresses above, the first is 7.09 blocks north of the temple and is on 700 East Street; the next is 23.92 blocks east of the temple on 4400 South Street (which is 44 blocks south of the temple), and the last is 13.32 blocks west of the temple on 7100 South Street (which is 71 blocks south of the temple).

The addresses immediately around the temple have a slightly more conventional naming scheme, but they still center on the temple. For example, the address of the Family History Library is 35 North West Temple. That tells you that the Library is .35 blocks north of the temple, and on West Temple Street. West Temple Street is the street that runs along the west side of the temple – also known as 100 West.

Once you understand the format, you will never need a map when looking for an address in Salt Lake City (or in most Utah towns, for that matter). In recent years it has been fashionable to name streets more conventional names, like Cherry Lane, Elm Street, etc. When faced with an incomprehensible address like 3145 South Maple Avenue, simply ask for the numbered street name of Maple Avenue, and you'll be told something like 2950 West. So now you know that the address on Maple

Avenue is 31.45 blocks south of the temple on 2950 West Street (29.5 blocks west of the temple).

FamilySearch

We've talked earlier in the book about the LDS Church's awesome genealogy website – **FamilySearch** *(www.familysearch.org)* that allows individuals to gain access to the genealogical resources that the LDS Church has gathered through the years. FamilySearch includes genealogical records for billions of individuals, from birth, death and marriage information to military records, census data, family histories, and much, much more. Like all other genealogical resources provided by the LDS Church, FamilySearch is available to anyone, regardless of religious affiliation.

The FamilySearch website was launched on May 24, 1999. From Day 1 it has been immensely popular – and incredibly busy. It gets roughly one million visitors *each day*. It has definitely positioned itself as one of the premier websites available to genealogists. Here's how it works: As you make a request for information, FamilySearch combs its extensive records, searching for matches on the name you entered. Not only that, it even matches last names that are spelled differently but sound the same (More/Moore, Fisher/Fischer, Smith/ Smythe, Meier/Meyer, etc.).

Matches on the surname (if it was a surname search) then have links to allow the researcher to learn more about the record. In most cases, a short description gives details about the information contained in the record. It may include information about dates and places of birth, parents, marriage and death information, as well as information about children.

When you go to *www.familysearch.org*, your first introduction will be to their home page. It provides an opportunity from its home page to begin your search immediately – you can enter information about the ancestor for whom you are searching, and off you go. Once you enter information specific to that ancestor, FamilySearch scours its databases for matches. It checks censuses, World War I and II draft registration cards, many marriage, birth, marriage and death databases, Social Security Death Index, etc. (actually, tons of et ceteras!).

Or, if you need a little help – whether you are a beginning genealogist or a crafty veteran, help is just a mouse click or two away. From the home page of FamilySearch, one of the options in the top tray is *Search*. Click on that and on the resulting drop-down box, click *Research Wiki*. In the upper-middle portion of the page, you'll see a search box titled, *Search by place or topic*. Enter some bit of information you would like to learn about. For example, perhaps you know that your great grandmother was born in Germany, but you don't have a clue about how to begin researching for her in Germany. In the *Search by place or topic* box, type *German Research*, and scan the results to see what might help you best. I did that, and received links to over 4,800 articles, Wikis, databases, passenger lists, etc., about German research. The first few hits were:

- German Genealogies
  - German Research Strategies
  - German Languages (German language and handwriting)
  - Schleswig-Holstein Research Websites
  - Germany Church and Civil Records
  - Getting Started with German Research

Or perhaps your needs are a little closer to home: you would like to know what Ohio birth records FamilySearch may have in their collection. Back in the *Search by place or topic* box, typing*Ohio birth records* yields over 1,000 hits, including these:

- Ohio birth Records (FamilySearch collection)
  - Ohio research Tips and Strategies

·Ohio Births and Christenings (FamilySearch Historical Records)
·How to Find Ohio Birth records

Clicking on one of the above items takes you to an article that explains about the FamilySearch collection, what is in it, what years the collections cover, and how to use the collection. It also provides some historical background about how and why the record or collection was gleaned.

Another of the tabs at the top of the FamilySearch home page says *Get Involved*. Click that, and in the drop-down box, select *Indexing*. This is your opportunity to give back to the genealogy world — the LDS Church is actively seeking volunteers to assist in indexing the scads of collections they have. If you have ever had to search a collection name-by-name, page by page because there was no index, you can appreciate how valuable this service is and how crucial it is to find volunteers! I have volunteered with the LDS Church, as well as with other organizations. When I did other organizations (okay — it was Ancestry.com), I've been able to index the records for the counties where my ancestors lived. It allowed me to streamline the search for ancestors and connections, but also allowed me to put in place a tool (the index for the records) for future genealogists to use.

For years (generations, actually), the LDS Church has been sending and continues to send volunteers all over the world to put family history records on microfilm. Millions of records are still on microfilm, fiche, and CDs, but the LDS Church is rapidly digitizing those records so that they will be available online.

FamilySearch Centers

Okay, so you don't live in the Rocky Mountain region of the United States, nor do you plan on going to Utah any time soon. Does that mean that you are out of luck, that all these fabulous records are simply tantalizingly outside your grasp? Fortunately for you and me, the answer is, "Of course not." The LDS Church has provided alternate access to all of their genealogical records via their *FamilySearch Centers* (formerly known as Family History Centers).

Considered branches to the FamilySearch Library in Salt Lake City, FamilySearch Centers are located literally throughout the world. Each is staffed by local volunteers who are interested in helping you conduct research on your family.

As of this printing, there are over 5,000 FamilySearch Centers spread throughout the world, operating in every state in the United States and in over 140 countries. And they are heavily used.

To determine whether there are any FamilySearch Centers near you (there almost certainly are), go to the LDS Church's genealogy website at www.familysearch.org/centers/locations, and you'll be taken to a map where all 5,000+ FamilySearch Centers can be found.

The hours of operation at the FamilySearch Centers vary from center to center. Since each center is staffed solely by volunteers, the hours are dependent on the volunteers' availability. Generally speaking, each FSC is open two or three days a week for anywhere from four to twelve hours on those days. The telephone numbers listed are generally for phones located within the Center; if you get no answer to your call, try at various times, especially in the evenings between 6:00pm and 9:00pm. Or you can merely stop by the address and if the center is not open, there is almost always a sign indicating the hours the FamilySearch Center is open. To narrow your time search, it is important to know that FamilySearch Centers are never open on Sundays or Mondays. If you do not have Internet access, call 866-406-1830 and representatives there will help identify the closest FamilySearch Center to you.

Each FamilySearch Center is also equipped with computers and Internet access so that you can access the many records available on CD as well as contact the LDS Church's genealogy website, www.familysearch.org.

As an added bonus, most FamilySearch Centers provide free access for subscription websites (like Ancestry.com, MyHeritage.com, FindMyPast.com, NewspaperArchive.com, Fold3.com, and others)

Getting the Most Out of Your Local FamilySearch Center

As wonderful as they are, FamilySearch Centers will be much more useful if you follow some basic guidelines.

Prepare

Before you go to your local FamilySearch Center, prepare for your visit. Have an idea about what line of your family (or what individual) you want to search for. Gather all the information you possibly can about the person or line that you want to research. Know surnames, city, county and/or state where they lived, and approximate dates of birth. The more information you can bring with you, the higher your likelihood of succeeding in your search.

Call Ahead

Before you just show up at one of the FamilySearch Centers near you, call the contact number and confirm the location and hours of operation. Because the Centers are staffed solely by volunteers, Center hours and days of operation may vary as volunteers come and go. The website might not have the latest information on hours of operation.

If you are not successful in reaching anyone at the telephone number listed on the website, don't give up. Contact one of the local congregations and they can put you in touch with someone who knows the times that the FamilySearch Center in that area operates.

Here's a hint: since all LDS church leaders serve on a voluntary basis, doing their church work around their regular 8:00am to 5:00pm jobs, the telephone numbers listed are often only answered on Sundays or weekday evenings, when these volunteer leaders are most likely to be at the church building.

Have Patience

Finally, have patience with those who staff these Centers. Few are professional genealogists; in fact, the vast majority are not. They are individuals like you, who have a great love of genealogy and family research and want to help others have successful research experiences. Let me stress that these Centers are open to anyone – regardless of religious belief – who has an interest in doing genealogy. In fact, records of attendance at these Centers indicate that something on the order of 60% of those who use FamilySearch Centers are not members of the Church of Jesus Christ of Latter-day Saints.

Share Your Success

As mentioned earlier in this chapter, the Genealogical Society of Utah and the LDS Church provides these wonderful resources for genealogists the world over. They are constantly adding to their collection. And that is where you come in. If you have had success in identifying ancestors through any of the LDS sources (or through any source, for that matter), please share that information with the LDS Church. It will become a part of their genealogical collection, which will in turn be available to other researchers who may be working on the same lines as you.

I have been contacted by genealogists as far away as Scotland who have gotten my name from genealogical information I had provided to the LDS church. It resulted in a new friend half a world away, and the sharing of more genealogical information between us.

Using the LDS Church Checklist

____FamilySearch Centers are great places to access the billions of genealogy records the Church of Jesus Christ of Latter-day Saints has.

____FamilySearch Centers are staffed by volunteers. Be patient with them.

____Prepare before you go to an FSC – the name or lines you want to research, and any information you may have on that person or line.

____You can locate an FSC nearest you by going to *www.familysearch.org/centers/locations*.

10

Genealogy Societies

You would expect that any hobby that has as many participants as genealogy does would have many organizations of likeminded people who get together and share their information and expertise. And so it is with genealogy. Literally thousands of genealogical organizations have sprung up through the years in support of this pastime. One or more of them may be just the answer you are looking for to help you find information on your family. And since some of them have been around in one form or another for as much as 150 years, the information they have gleaned on their family lines is often extensive.

A visit to the Internet confirms the existence of these societies, and their willingness to share their information and expertise. While I was writing this book, I typed "genealogy society" on **Google,** and it yielded over 26 *million*(!) hits. Some are area-specific (e.g., Germany, Hancock County, Maine, San Mateo, etc.) and others are family-specific. Some are societies that just provide information, support and expertise to their members. When I Googled genealogical societies, the first site among that 26 million was rightfully the **National Genealogical Society** (*www.ngsgenealogy.org*). It is a great organization to know about and to use. In 2020 this large genealogical organization merged with another huge genealogical organization — the **Federation of Genealogical Societies**, and the merged entity now boasts over 500,000 members and over 500 family associations and genealogy societies in its membership. By searching for these societies on the Internet, you can find out about their existence, mail and/or e-mail address, as well any website and telephone numbers that are available.

Membership in most of the genealogical societies is the modest cost of annual dues (generally in the range of $15 to $35 per year; NGS is $75 / year). The dues may include access to family or area genealogical information as well as a newsletter focusing on genealogical aspects of the family or region. These societies can be of great assistance to genealogists.

Several years ago while doing research for another book, I ran across a list of genealogy societies. Scanning it quickly, I noticed the Hudson Family Association listed there. My grandmother was a Hudson, and despite a number of efforts to learn more about her line, I knew virtually nothing about the family beyond her grandfather's name. So almost as an afterthought, I jotted down the address, and a few days later I fired off a short letter:

Dear Hudson Family Association,

I came across your organization in Moore's Book of Lists. My grandmother is a Hudson, so I would like to join your organization. The entry in the book didn't have much information about your society, but I am enclosing $50 for dues. If that is too much, please send me as many back issues of your newsletter as the extra amount will purchase.

Thank you,
Daniel Quillen

I am by nature an optimist, so I was cautiously optimistic that the Hudson Family Association would be able to assist me in my Hudson ancestral pursuit. Within days I received a note welcoming me to the Hudson Family Association. They explained that the association was formed to further genealogical research on the family line, and asked whether I would be willing to share information about my side of the family.

I was happy to share the information (most genealogists are like that!) and I shared what I knew of my Hudson line, as scanty as it was. I shared birth and marriage information about my current family, my grandmother, her parents and her paternal grandfather's name and place of birth.

I was totally unprepared for the amount and quality of assistance they gave me. A few weeks after I sent my letter, I received my first copy of the *Bulletin Hudsoniana*, the Hudson Family Association newsletter. One section was devoted to welcoming new members. Imagine my unbounded joy when I found the following entry:

Welcome New Members!
   Quillen, W. Daniel:
   William Daniel QUILLEN, born _____, Lynwood, Los Angeles, CA married 13 April 1979 Bonita BLAU;
   Versie Lee LOWRANCE, born McClain, OK, married 13 July 1951 William Edgar QUILLEN, born Norman, OK;
   Alma HUDSON, born 24 Apr 1913, Stephens, OK, married 5 Oct 1932 Elzie Lee LOWRANCE, born 24 Feb 1906, Wayne, OK;
   Francis Marion HUDSON, born 13 Nov 1877, Pope, AR, died 12 Jan 1960, Los Angeles, CA, married 1909 Margaret Ellen TURPIN;
   Jeremiah HUDSON, born 1851, AR, died 1914, Dibble, OK, married about 1873 Frances DUVALL, AR;
   Francis Marion HUDSON, born 20 March 1829, Lauderdale County,

AL, married about 1848 Mary _____;

Jeremiah HUDSON, living 1830 in Lauderdale County, AL, married Lavina JONES, living in 1830 in Lauderdale County, AL; Levi HUDSON, married Hannah ____;

Major HUDSON, born about 1690, died 16 Nov. 1781, Worchester County, MD, married Martha GILLETT;

Henry HUDSON, born 8 July 1669, Somerset County, Maryland, died 24 Dec 1720, Somerset County, MD married (1) _____ LUDLONG?, (2) Ellis DENNIS;

Henry HUDSON, born about 1642, Accomack County, Virginia, died about 1710, Somerset County, Maryland, married about 1664 Lydia SMITH;

Richard HUDSON, born 1605, England, died about 1657, Northampton County, Virginia, married (1) Mary _____, married (2) Mrs. Mary HAYES, married (3) Barbara JACOBS;

William HUDSON, born about 1570, London, England, married about 1603 Alice Turner;

Henry HUDSON, born about 1541

They had taken the scant information I had provided them and tied me back in a direct line of ancestors to 1541 – 13 generations and 450+ years! A subsequent request from me provided Family Group Sheets on every family member along with documentation of many of the names and dates – hundreds of names and a great deal of vital statistic information.

You'll note, by the way, that much of the Hudson family information that was provided to me was unknown, especially the further I climbed the family tree. In a number of instances, there are first names only, or missing dates, or at best approximated dates. That's okay – at least I have information to go on that will help me find some of these people later on. Notwithstanding the missing or approximated information, it was a wonderful find indeed.

Can you take one more story? My third great grandfather, Leonidas Horney, was a Colonel in the Civil War. He had also been a bit of a prominent citizen in Schuyler County, Illinois, serving as county surveyor, a prosperous farmer and served as a bit of a war correspondent for his hometown paper while he was serving in the War.

A few years ago, I learned of a genealogical society in his home town of Rushville, Schuyler county. Their website listed the cost and advantages of becoming a member:

Membership for the Schuyler Jail Museum & Genealogical Society is $15.00 yearly (due in January).

Membership includes 4 issues of the Schuylerite. *They are mailed twice a year — Spring & Summer together & Fall & Winter together.*

The Schuylerite *– quarterly publication, averaging 44 pages per issue. This is all historical and genealogical information! Back issues contain marriage indexes, probate and cemetery records, schools and class attendance, social events from early records, obits, family histories....*

The Volunteers of the society will provide research for you at $5.00 per hour plus 25 cents a copy for genealogy data they have at the research center. (Bolding *added) If you are needing research done please write to the society at the above address.*

The research fee of $5 an hour really caught my eye (what a bargain!), and I sent a check for $100 and asked them to send me whatever they found about him.

A few weeks later, I was gratified to receive a copy of the daybook (journal / diary) he kept during the Mexican-American War, which he served in as a private. The journal had many snippets that told me about this ancestor of mine (more on him and this journal a little later).

Definitely see if you can locate information about genealogical societies established in the areas where your ancestors lived. Or –

genealogical societies focused on a particular surname, like my Hudson Family Association mentioned earlier.

I share these stories to assure you that no matter how alone you may feel in your research at times, there are often many people out there who have already found the very information you are searching for. And the best part about that message is that they are almost always willing to share that information.

Genealogy societies provide a variety of valuable services, including:

·Timely how-to advice on research for the family or in a particular area.

·They share, share, share information (that's how I got all that information on the Hudson line).

·Preserve and make available records (many societies get involved with microfilming and indexing original records for their members).

·Making your ancestors come alive by providing stories from their lives. Some are humorous, some historical, many are tragic. All serve to help you become better acquainted with your ancestors.

·Recommendations for improving your genealogy research through the announcement (or sponsoring) of seminars or the publication of articles.

·Evaluations of hardware and software used for genealogical purposes.

OLLEY OLLEY OXEN FREE!

Searching for your ancestors is often a little like playing hide-and-go-seek with your four- or five-year-old little brother. He loves the game, but doesn't quite get the rules. Giggling or moving, he seems to delight in being found.

And so it is with many of your ancestors – it seems they often do all they can to be found. As you work (play!) in genealogy, you'll be surprised at how much information will come to you – almost as though by accident. Through the years I have found that the smallest amount of effort on my part often yields immense genealogical success. Anyone who has done much genealogy at all has multiple stories of amazing coincidences that resulted in genealogical progress – chance meetings with genealogists working on their line, intuitional feelings leading to information in least-expected places, etc.

Don't get me wrong – there are still those ancestors out there that seem to be extremely good at playing hide-and-go-seek. Unlike the little brother mentioned at the outset of this section, they are experts at hiding and dodging even your best efforts. They will bring out your best detective instincts! In the mean time, keep looking! If all else fails, try calling, "Olley olley oxen free!" to see if they will reveal their hiding places.

Genealogy Societies Checklist
____Determine which surnames you wish to do research on.

____Seek out websites and books that cover Genealogical Societies – whether location- or family-surname specific.

____Be prepared to share what you know about your family.

____Be persistent.

Additional Resources

Meyer, Mary Keysor, *Meyer's Directory of Genealogical Societies in the USA and Canada,* Libra Publications, 11th edition. (May 1996/1997)

Check out the National Genealogical Society site: *www.ngsgenealogy.org.* You
can become a member, or use many of their free resources available on their
website.

11

Tools of the Trade – The Internet

The Internet has touched almost all aspects of our society, and it has proven to be a huge blessing for genealogists. Complementary computer software has been designed specifically to assist genealogists in capturing and organizing the information they find through their research.

To illustrate the power I speak of, try this experiment: Go to the Internet, and using whichever search engine you are most familiar with (Google it, so to speak!), type in your last name (or the last name of an ancestor) and the word *genealogy*, and click on *Search*. I did this for a number of my lines, and I averaged a little over a million hits per surname.

Of course...a million+ hits can be overwhelming...but I can narrow it significantly by adding information like first and last names. When I searched the Internet using the phrase "William L. McCollough married Lucy Arabella Phillips," I received (only) 7,400 hits.

Each one of these hits has the potential of yielding information about a family member for whom you have been searching in vain. And more often than not, the information doesn't stop there – my experience is that once I find one person in this manner, there are often two, three or more generations beyond that included in the listing.

Genealogy Websites

The Internet is the largest genealogy library in the world. We've already talked about some of the top search websites – Ancestry.com and FamilySearch.org, but listed below are some of my other favorite and most productive genealogy websites, and a little about each of them.

Findagrave – this great (and free) website (*FindaGrave.com*) has gathered over 225 *million* memorials of deceased individuals. And all this work has been done by volunteers all over the world. Typically, the memorials include birth and death dates and places, as well as the cemetery the individual was buried in. Most of the memorials (95%+, I'd guess) have photographs of the individual's tombstone, and often will include a death certificate, obituary, picture of the individual, etc. – all added by volunteers, family members, and others. The memorials will also frequently list links to the memorials of the person's parents, spouse(s) and children.

Following is the link to the Findagrave memorial for my great grandmother, Emma Adelia Sellers Cunningham: *www.findagrave.com/memorial/36792312/emma-adelia-cunningham*. Take a look, and you can see what kinds of information are often included in these memorials. I have used Findagrave to overcome many (many!) genealogical brick walls though the years – including discovering the maiden name of many women. You can see why I love this website.

(By the way, my Emma Adelia graces the cover of this book with my great grandfather!)

I use Findagrave all the time in my research – it is marked as one of my "favorites" on my Internet browser.

Fold3.com — this is the "military arm" of Ancestry.com. As that implies, Fold3.com focuses its efforts primarily on military records. I have used it extensively through the years, when looking for military records of my military ancestors, and I have not been disappointed. A subscription runs $7.95 per month, or $79.95 for an annual subscription.

Newspapers.com — this is another of the genealogy services that is part of the Ancestry.com family. It has been a remarkable resource for me to find members of my family that I would have otherwise overlooked. It has also provided information on my ancestors such as obituaries — which often list great detail about my ancestors, as well as information about their parents, spouse, children, etc. It is available for as little as $7.95 per month ($44.95 for six months) for the basic plan, and $19.90 per month / $74.90 for six months. If you've purchased the most expensive Ancestry.com plan, the basic Newspapers.com subscription is included.

Ellis Island website. You already know I absolutely love the power of this website for my immigrant ancestors, and I gave you plenty of details in an earlier chapter.

Random Acts of Genealogical Kindness – this is one of my favorite genealogy sites on the Internet! I think it symbolizes the values of genealogical generosity that most genealogists are known for. The website is *www.raogk.org*, and I guarantee you will find it to your liking. Genealogy volunteers from all over the world offer their services – to photograph tombstones, go to local government offices to search for records, etc. They respond to requests from other genealogists to find genealogical information. It was down for a few years, but has recently started back up again. They have nearly 1,000 volunteers – and could use some more — check them out!

Cyndi's List of Genealogy Sites on the Internet (*www.cyndislist.com*). Cyndi's List provides links to other genealogy websites. Once you find a website that catches your interest, click on the link and you are there. It is user friendly, and is a great place to begin your free on-line research. Cyndi's List has over 320 million links to various and sundry genealogy websites!

There are a number of genealogy companies / websites that offer advanced research capabilities for those willing to pay a subscription fee. Two of the best known are **MyHeritage** (*www.MyHeritage.com*) and **Ancestry.com** (*www.Ancestry.com*). They are sites that offer subscribers a variety of databases through which they can comb in search of their ancestors. Each, along with FamilySearch, has access to billions of genealogy records.

Ancestry.com is the 800-pound gorilla in the genealogy world (although MyHeritage is close on their heels). They have billions of records available to their subscribers. Annual packages at Ancestry run between $250 and $600 per year depending on the package you select. They also offer monthly and six-month rates. But – if you are really getting into genealogy, it may be worth it. MyHeritage.com is also a subscription service. As of this writing, their subscription price $199 for the first year, and $299 for subsequent years. Both are available to use for free at LDS FamilySearch Centers. Also, both Ancestry and MyHeritage offer free two-week trials.

Another well-regarded subscription service is **FindMyPast.com**. They also have billions of records for genealogists to access. The cost of their subscription is between MyHeritage's and Ancestry's ($20 to $30 per month). FindMyPast is focused primarily on British and Irish genealogy, but they do have some North American records.

As we've discussed, I think one of the best free research sites to consider is **FamilySearch.org**. I've mentioned it and have used it to share examples of how to use it throughout the book. They also have access to a billion+ genealogy records. The LDS Church also has FamilySearch Centers all over the world in many of their local meeting houses. They are staffed by volunteers, so their hours vary from place to place, depending on who is volunteering. In the FamilySearch Centers, genealogists can access all the records of FamilySearch.org, as well as use Ancestry.com for no cost. And – the good news is that most FamilySearch Centers have access to each of the subscription services I've mentioned in the past few paragraphs, and you are able to use them to your heart's content!

The four genealogy websites I use most often are Ancestry.com, Newspapers.com, FamilySearch.org, and Findagrave.com. The first two require subscriptions, and the latter two are free. I use the others listed on this page from time to time, but these are the main resources I use — and I use them frequently.

Genealogy Websites Checklist

____Familiarize yourself with the various websites mentioned in this chapter (Findagrave, Cyndi's List, Ancestry.com, FamilySearch.org, etc.).

____Use those sites to further your genealogical research.

____If you don't have access to some of the subscription sites (Ancestry.com, Newspapers.com, etc.), you can use some of them for free at LDS FamilySearch Centers. There should be one nearby where you live (there are over 5,000 operating in over 140 countries!).

Additional Resources

____Genealogy services Internet providers continually refresh and upgrade their offerings and number of records they have available. Google "Top Ten Genealogy Sites" every now and then, to see if a newcomer has stepped up that you'd like to try out.

12

Genealogy Software

There are dozens of software packages available on the market today that will help you keep your genealogical research organized.

So what should you look for when you finally decide to organize all your manual and paper records into a software program? The first and foremost thing I think is important is user friendliness. No matter how powerful your genealogy program is or how much storage space it has, if you don't understand how to use it, it is of no real use to you.

Following are some of the more popular and capable genealogy programs out there, any one of which I recommend:

Family Tree Builder (by My Heritage) is one of the most powerful genealogy software packages on the market. It is considered one of the best all-purpose software packages for genealogists, and receives award after award in the industry. Its user interface is especially customer-friendly (one of my needs / requirements!), and it offers a large array of features – probably more than you'll ever need! Check them out at *www.myheritage.com/family-tree-builder*.

Legacy Family Tree is another of the powerful yet affordable genealogy software programs out there. It comes standard with many of the features its competitors have, but this software is exceptionally intuitive. It is the package I use, because the user interface is easy and serves me well. Like many of its competitors, it has a wide range of capabilities and features. Learn more about them at *legacyfamilytree.com*.

Family Historian software has gained a strong following among genealogists in recent years, because of its powerful capabilities, user-friendly interface, and its ability to create detailed family trees. You can learn about them at *www.family-historian.co.uk*.

Ancestral Quest is another of those powerful genealogy software packages available to genealogists. It is available from some retail outlets as well as Ancestral Quest's website at *www.ancquest.com*.

Ultimate Family Tree is a great, popular, and user-friendly genealogy program. Developed and marketed by The Learning Company, it is considered a very well-rounded software package, garnering high marks from users for its charts, reports and publishing capabilities. It is available from many retail outlets and Amazon.com.

Genealogical Research and Analysis Management Programming System. Okay, so the name of this software package doesn't exactly roll off your tongue, but its acronym does: GRAMPS. This is a package that helps you create family trees. One of the best things about this package is it is completely free. Most of these other packages offer a free version (or at least a free trial), but GRAMPS is completely free. It has a lot of features, but one of them is *not* ease of use. So – since you are just beginning your genealogical adventure, you might pass on GRAMPS until you have a little more experience under your belt (or if you're a techy)!

All of these genealogy software packages are very similar. I think the differences are minimal between packages, and you should find the one that you feel most at ease with – the one that has the most comfortable user interface for you.

All these software packages (except GRAMPS) are in the range of $25 to $50, depending on which versions you purchase.

Genealogy Software Checklist

_____Check out genealogy packages on Amazon, read the reviews, and decide which package will work best for you.

____Google *Top Ten Genealogy Software Packages*, and see what the experts have to say about the latest and greatest software packages out there.

____Focus on customer reviews regarding ease of use / customer-friendliness.

13

Help Your Descendants — Write a Personal History and Keep a Journal!

Consider the following scenario: You are helping your grandmother clean out the attic of her old Victorian home, and while working you discover a dusty old book in one corner of the attic. Taking it into the light, you open it and discover that it is a personal history that your 2nd great grandfather had written near the end of his life. As you scan its pages, you realize that he provided detailed information about his life and its joys and challenges as well as his hopes and dreams. Included on its old yellowed pages you find information about his parents, his sweetheart and each of his children. As a bonus, he wrote about various and sundry items that were happening on the national scene: a presidential election (and who he favored and why), how the family was weathering an economic downturn, his views on various wars or conflicts the country was involved in, etc.

What a find! What a joy that would be for you! Now - have you considered that you have it within your power to provide that very same information to your own descendants? If you wrote a personal history or perhaps even kept a daily (or weekly or monthly) journal, it could be your genealogical gift to your posterity. With a little bit of effort on your part, such a document could preserve important genealogical information for your children, grandchildren and beyond. It could provide a peek into your soul if you share your feelings and thoughts about the life around you.

Writing a Personal History

I have to make a confession: I started writing a personal history at least a half dozen times before I finally found a formula that worked and allowed me to finish it. But like so many other things that are worthwhile, sometimes persistence is the greatest asset you can have to accomplish something – but a formula helps too.

After trying several different methods, I finally hit on a pretty simple and successful one. Following are the steps I followed to successfully complete my personal history:

·Write down a list of "chapters" that you would like to have in your personal history.
·Under each chapter heading, write a list of experiences or information that should be included in that chapter.
·Decide on a time during the week that you will write on a regular basis.
·Decide whether you want to include photographs in your history.
·Begin writing.
·Continue writing.
·Just do it!

Chapters

Begin your personal history by writing down a list of chapter headings. This will be the beginning of your personal history. If you are like me, the number of chapters will grow as you think of experiences that do not fit neatly into an existing chapter; when that happens, just start another chapter heading. Don't just write the chapters down in a Table of Contents, but write them on separate pages of a pad of paper or separate them by page breaks if you are using a computer.

Next, spend a few minutes with each chapter and write down a list of everything you think should go into that chapter. Don't worry about having an exhaustive list to begin with – I can tell you from experience that as you write your history, additional memories will come to you. When that happens, pause in your writing and go to whichever chapter the experience you just remembered belongs in, and jot down a few lines – just enough to remember what it was about so you can write about it later. If it doesn't fit into any of the chapters you've written down, then start a new chapter, and put that first memory in it. Then return to the chapter you were writing in.

Below is a list of chapters that eventually ended up in my personal history. It is certainly not an exhaustive list, but the one that applied to my life:

- Summary
- Genealogy
- Birth
- The early years
- Schooling years
- College
- Friends
- Marriage
- Children
- Employment
- Memorable vacations
- Significant people in my life
- Significant personal events
- Significant world events

·Dan on Dan (my thoughts about me)

You will doubtless have other chapters that I do not have: military service, famous people you've known, my political career, My Life as a Spy, etc. Now take each chapter and list events you want to be sure and include in your history, like this:

Memorable vacations:
  ·Disneyland
  ·Camping at Mt. Shavano
  ·Yellowstone
  ·Sand dunes
  ·The beach in San Diego
  ·Disney World
  ·Western Europe
  ·Ireland
  ·Scotland
  ·Etc.

Significant world events:
  ·Man walking on the moon
  ·Kennedy assassination
  ·Nixon resignation
  ·The Challenger explosion
  ·The Gulf War
  ·The Berlin Wall comes down
  ·Clinton impeachment
  ·Trump Impeachment
  ·Bush/Gore photo-finish presidential election
  ·9/11
  ·Etc.

And what about the technological advances that have occurred during your lifetime? Some of the most significant technological developments in the history of the world have occurred in the last few decades:
- Cell phones
- Microwave ovens
- Blackberries
- The Internet (what would we do without that!?)
- Pop Tarts
- Digital clocks
- Computers (depending on your age!)
- Laptop computers
- Tablets
- Electric cars
- Etc.

Several years ago, a genealogist friend – a distant cousin – and I formed a friendship through our common ancestor – her second great grandfather was my third great grandfather, Leonidas Horney. Somehow, she had discovered the existence of a series of letters he had written to his wife, and she compiled them into a book. The letters – now a sort of journal / personal history of his life at that time — detailed his exploits during the Civil War, giving counsel on when to sell the agricultural products they were raising (including a caution to only accept gold or silver, and not "worthless paper money,") and counsel to his children (for the boys: practice writing two hours each day). He also mentioned several crucial things about the political leadership of the day, and his thoughts about conducting the Civil War:

·**Secesshes:** He was angry with the *Secesshes* (as he called them – meaning the Secessionists) for leaving the Union;

·**Southern hospitality:** He said the citizens they met while marching through the south were good people and kind to them;

·**Abolitionists**: Although he agreed that slavery must end so the Union could be preserved, he felt the rhetoric and antagonism of the Northern abolitionist movements were causing the war to be unnecessarily extended;

·**Slave recruits**: When it was announced that former slaves were going to be allowed into the Union army, he felt some of the Union soldiers wouldn't fight alongside them. As for himself, he wrote that if they were willing to fight, he was willing to fight beside them.

·**Lincoln**: Although he lived less than sixty miles from Springfield, Illinois, where Abraham Lincoln was from, and was able to hear him speak several times, he did not like Lincoln — *at all*. He considered himself a "Douglas Man," (Stephen Douglas – Lincoln's opponent in the 1860 presidential election). In one of his letters home, he spoke of his loathing for Lincoln, and labeled him the "laughingstock of the whole world."

Such personal and contemporary insights about this terrible time in our nation's history was absolutely fascinating for me to read, and gave me insights to this military ancestor of mine.

Back to *your* personal history — again, the reason for these lists (potential chapters, things to include in your chapters, etc.) is just to provide a memory jogger for when you begin your own writing. Don't worry about making it an exhaustive list – just write down what comes to mind now. I guarantee you that more ideas will come as you begin writing. When they do, just pause your writing, go to the Chapter you think they belong, and write a short bullet point on the topic, so you don't lose it.

Set a Regular Time

Once you have written down your chapters and have a list of events to write about under each chapter, it's time to set your writing schedule. Few individuals have the time or ability to sit down and write their personal history from beginning to end. Life happens to interrupt that plan for most of the people I know.

If possible, select a time that works best in your schedule. In my case, I decided to write every Sunday afternoon for a few hours. I decided to do it within an hour of returning from church services each Sunday. Some Sundays things came up and I was not able to write; but generally I was able to put in at least one or two hours each Sunday afternoon, occasionally more. Within a year, I had a completed personal history. Perhaps this time will work for you, or maybe it is an entirely different day of the week or time of the day. Regardless, the important thing is to set aside a day and time and then stick to it.

Additional Help

There are a goodly number of books on the market today that will guide you to look at your life and have a number of questions that will spark memories and help you begin writing your personal history. I have listed a few of the better ones at the end of this chapter in the *Additional Resources* section.

Keep a Journal

While writing a personal history is like writing the Reader's Digest version of your life, keeping a daily, weekly, or monthly journal is more like writing the original text. I say a "daily, weekly, or monthly journal" because it is my personal experience that with life's pace these days, it is very difficult to set aside time each day to keep a journal. But as with writing your personal history, I believe that if you set aside a set time each week, or perhaps each month (like the first Sunday of each month) to write in a journal, you will be more successful than if you try to write every day. If you also write entries for significant events – new jobs, the birth of your children, significant national events, etc. – then you will capture many important things that will be of interest to your children and others.

I have kept a journal for nearly five decades, although I must admit, not as faithfully as I would like. But it has already borne wonderful fruit for our family. For example, when our children were still living at home and we celebrated each of our their birthdays, they enjoyed hearing my wife and I read what we wrote about them in our journals on the day of their birth. We wrote about what the day was like, the kind of birthing room, how long labor was, the doctor's name, and our feelings about each new child we welcomed into the world. (Even the teenagers liked to hear these stories time and again.)

Each year on New Year's Day (or shortly thereafter), I write a "State of the World" and "State of the Quillen Family" entry. It includes what is going on in the world and nation, who the president of the United States is (and my thoughts about him), and those kinds of things. Then I write about our family – my employment situation, including my salary, what each of the family members is doing, and relatively mundane details about our life: the value of our home, our house payment, the cost of groceries (the price of a gallon of milk, a pound of hamburger and butter, etc.) and the cost of gas. Already it is fun for me to look back and read about times in our early marriage. I am amazed at how nervous we were to step up to the $356 per month house payment for our first home, for example. Imagine what my great grandchildren will think when they read those same words. And don't you wish you had a daily – or even weekly or monthly - journal of one of your ancestors from 100 years ago?

In a daily journal, I suggest that you share your feelings and thoughts about things. Share your deep love for your sweetheart and your children, share your concerns, challenges and disappointments. Celebrate your successes and your joys.

In the *Military Records* chapter, I left a teaser about my third great-grandfather's journal – the "Daybook" that a genealogy society researcher had discovered in her search for information about this ancestor of mine.

He kept the journal only for the first part of his service: from July 22, 1846 to September 26, 1846. Two months in the life of this 29-year-old military ancestor of mine. Included in the pages are many weather-related entries ("Cool wind from the north," and "...hot all day..."), how many deer they saw and killed when they hunted for their Company, the names of and amount of money lent to four fellow soldiers, the size of grape vines he saw, the high costs he encountered in San Antonio during his trek: corn ($1 a bushel), whiskey (10 cents per drink), 25 cents for a small apple pie, $1 a gallon for molasses. He also took the time to notate the miles they marched or sailed between points.

He described some of the women he saw in some of the frontier towns they traveled through (his original spelling is preserved!): "Some few of the...women are very handsome but are mostly the rechedest things that could be immagined, especialy the old ones."

Someone had (thankfully!) transcribed his journal (he and I share poor handwriting – perhaps it's genetic?).

There was a bit or irony in his journal that he would never be aware of. On July 22, 1846, one of his entries read:

4.00 (hours) from Memphis to Vicksburgh (probably by train, horse or wagon)

3.50 (hours) from Vicksburgh to Natchez

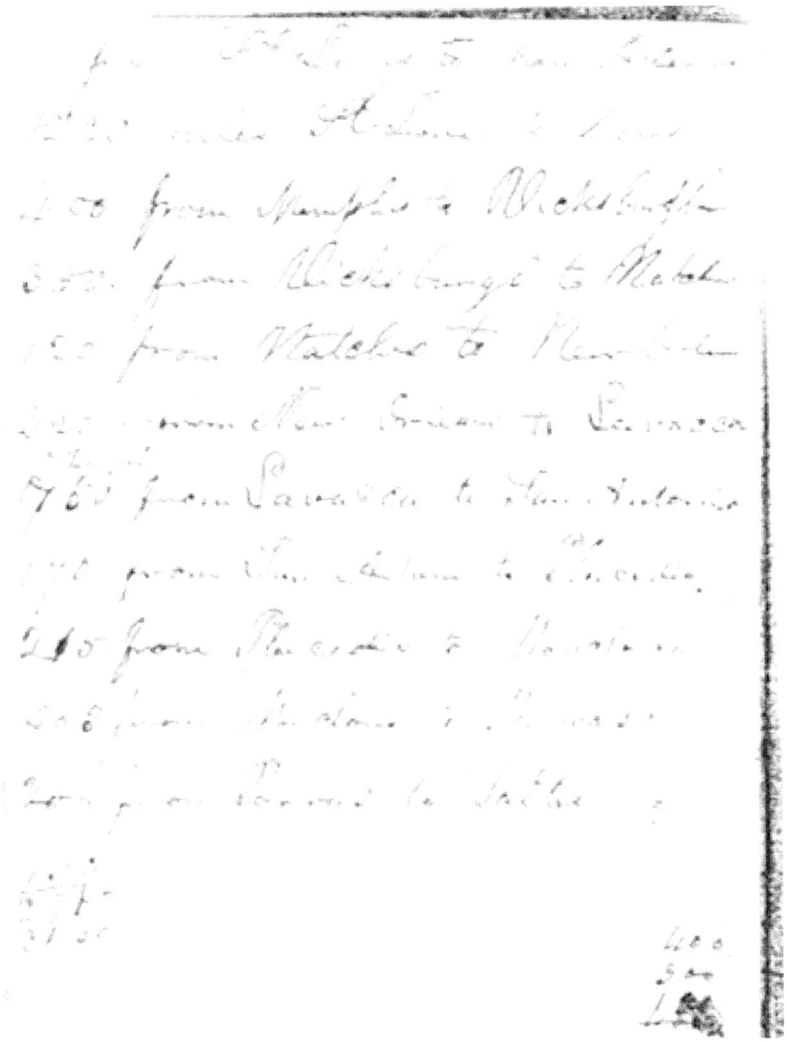

Just shy of seventeen years later, on May 16, 1863, Colonel Leonidas Horney was killed at a battle that was part of the siege of Vicksburg — Champion Hill.

But let me tell you – I loved, loved, loved reading his journal entries and getting to know him a bit through his journal pages.

What Do I Do Now?

Okay – so you have taken my advice and written a personal history. Now what do you do with it? You can leave it on your computer and risk losing it in the next hard drive crash, but there is much more that you can do with it. After I finished mine, I made copies of it and gave it to each of my family members. I used a self-publishing company and had my history bound into book form, ordering enough copies for myself, my parents and sisters, our children and an estimated number for *their* children. The cost for thirty books was a little over $1,000.

But — You don't have to go to all that expense – you have several alternatives to what I had at the time I finished my personal history. The cheap-and-easy way is to have your history printed and spiral bound at a local copy store, or simply put it in a three-ring binder.

Or – you can use Amazon.com's just-in-time printing capabilities. This method requires you to upload your front and back covers and a pdf of the contents. Give it a price. Then you post it on Amazon.com. When you're ready to print copies, just order them like you would any other book, and *voila* – you don't print more copies than you need, and the process is quite simple.

To use Amazon to print and distribute your book, go to this website: *blog.reedsy.com/guide/kdp/how-to-publish-a-book-on-amazon/*. They will give you a step-by-step process. It's relatively easy...I often have a difficult time with technology, and I was able to do this the first time with no problems for this book! The only caveat is you'll need front and back covers. The Reedsy website listed earlier in this paragraph will give you some templates to choose a cover from. You'll have to upload a picture or graphic, though. If you have one that is suitable – great. If not, you'll need to have someone create a cover for you. One of the sites I'm familiar with (and have used and can recommend) for cover design is www.canva.com. After you've created an account on Canva, (it's free), you'll come to the *Dashboard*. Click the three dots above *More*, and one of the selections is *Cover Designs* – that's where you can begin creating your cover. Once you've created and saved your cover, you will use the cover later as you work your way through the Reedsy / Kindle Direct Publishing (KDP) website mentioned at the beginning of this paragraph.

If you're uncomfortable creating a book cover design from Canva.com, you can hire a cover designer at Upwork (*www.Upwork.com*) or The Urban Writers (*TheUrbanWriters.com*). Cover designs from these places can be as little as $25 or as much as several hundred dollars.

I mentioned above that when I finished my history I gave copies to my family members. I am of course not actually finished – I have had many experiences since I completed my history nearly twenty years ago. So I titled my history *W. Daniel Quillen – the First Fifty-ish Years*, and I intend to write additional volumes (perhaps every decade) after that.

By the way, the method I am suggesting for writing your personal history would work very well for writing a biography of an aging relative. If they are not going to do it themselves, this would make a great formula for eliciting the information from them so that you could write it for them.

Here is the front cover of my life story; I used a graphic artist friend to design it, before I knew about Canva or Reedsy.

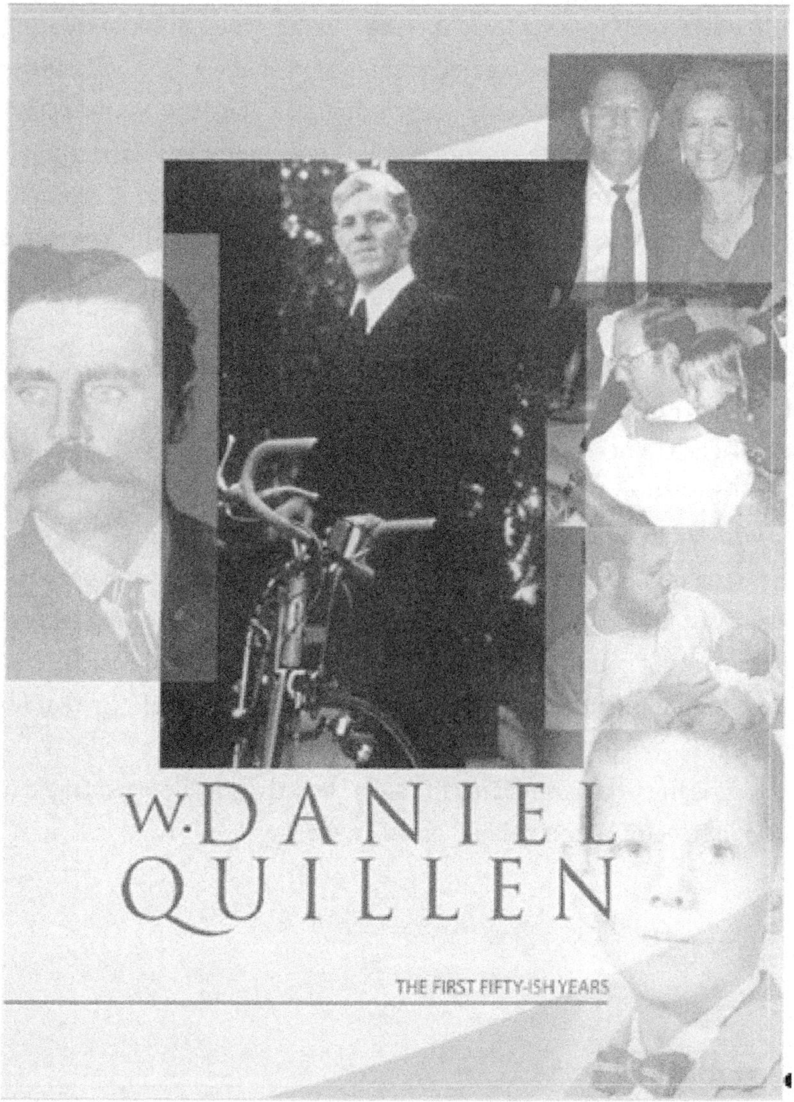
W. DANIEL
QUILLEN
THE FIRST FIFTY-ISH YEARS

Help Your Descendants! Checklist

____Decide whether you want to write your own personal history.

____Begin the process by writing down the chapters you think best represent the major aspects of your life. Write each chapter name on a separate piece of paper.

____Under each chapter heading, write a list of the events that should be covered in that chapter.

____Determine a time that will work best in your schedule for you to write your personal history.

____Purchase a journal

____Determine how often you want to write

____Begin writing!

____Continue writing!

Additional Resources

Green, Bob, and Fulford, D. G., *To Our Children's Children: Preserving Family Histories for Generations to Come*, Doubleday Publishing. (March 1993)

14

Kids & Genealogy

"Whatchya doin', Mom?"
"Oh, just a little genealogy."
"Okay.....Can I help?" One way or another, this conversation occurs time and again in the homes of many genealogists. I hear frequently from readers of my books that their children are interested in doing some genealogy, and they wonder if I have any tips or pointers on how to get them started.

Boy, do I ever!

First of all, I think questions in and interest about genealogy are quite natural for children of genealogists – they see you or your spouse (or both!) spending lots of your discretionary time searching for your ancestors. Your obvious interest is intriguing to them, and they wish to participate also.

The youth of this generation are like no others in their technical capability and aptitude. Young and nimble fingers and thumbs, practiced at texting and typing, are a natural fit for the genealogist's trade. Their understanding of search engines and the ability to get the most out of them is unrivaled. About a dozen years ago I visited my sister and her family in Alaska. They are a wired family, even then (they still are!) – not only did Mom and Dad have I-pads, but so did both of their children – ages 9 and 4 at the time of this incident. I had come for a visit, and was enjoying my time with them. I watched in utter amazement as Chase, my sister's precocious four-year-old son, navigated around his I-pad. His fingers fairly flew over the touch screen, finding and opening apps more quickly than my old brain could even comprehend.

I have since reflected on that…my earliest memories begin when I was about Chase's age. Those memories are filled with Lincoln Logs, Tinker Toys and Tonka trucks. Computers were still housed in very large rooms!

All that to say – I think your children (and grandchildren), from a very young age, are likely to be very adept at doing genealogy, and I am a big fan of getting them involved as soon as they begin showing interest. Following are some of my thoughts on activities that might be great for your children to begin participating in, whether they are pre-teens or teenagers. As they develop their skills (and mature a bit), they can expand their interests and work into more research-based genealogical activities.

Grandma & Grandpa

An often-overlooked genealogical generation is the one closest to us: our parents – your children's grandparents. I think a wonderful activity for your children would be to learn all they can about Grandpa and Grandma. Whether the information sessions are via personal visits, telephone, FaceTime, or Zoom calls, both your children and their grandparents will enjoy this activity.

In about their middle school years, all our children were required to do some genealogical research for one of their classes. A favorite subject of their information gathering was my wife's father – a veteran of World War II. He patiently answered their questions, and enjoyed the one-on-one time he had with these descendants of his.

As a teenager, I asked my grandfather if he remembered the first time he saw an automobile. He relished the opportunity to tell me that the first time he and his father saw an automobile in the rural farm country of Oklahoma, the noisy creature scared their horses so bad that they had an impromptu rodeo, and then a quick tour of their neighbor's corn field – wagon and all. While my grandfather thought the automobile a fabulous sight, the horses weren't so sure!

Years later, this same grandfather joined me in touring the Smithsonian. When we got to the Industrial section (a section I probably would have blown right past), he delighted in showing me large farm machinery similar to machines his father had, and he regaled me with memories about working with the machinery, which was at times balky in turn-of-the-20th century America.

It also occurred to me that a young rural lad's first horse was probably akin to my first car. Yep – such was the case. Even though he was in his 80s when we were speaking about it, he still remembered the name of that first horse, the kind of horse it was; its temperament, gait, etc. He also confirmed that youth that got old sway-backed nags as first horses were keenly aware they were riding that generation's battered Gremlin or Yugo!

If your children are interested, equip them with appropriate recording devices to capture the words of these relatives so close to them on the family tree. Whether audio or video recordings, they will be something to cherish for a long time – both as the relatives interviewed depart this life, as well as being a nostalgic look and listen back to your child in years to come.

Census Research

I have thought a lot about whether or not youth can be successful in searching for ancestors in census records. While I don't think it is an activity suitable to pre-teens, I think most teens would be able to handle the research and diligence required to search for and locate family members in censuses.

Censuses are full of family information, and with completed indexes, they provide a great feel-good search experience for beginning (and more experienced!) genealogists.

So, with just a little tutoring and guidance, I think teens can become tremendous census researchers. As they find family members on the censuses, encourage them to capture the information, either through printing census sheets, or by completing census forms that are available online (as mentioned earlier: fillable forms are available for free at *www.ngsgenealogy.org*).

Indexing

Another genealogical activity youth can be involved in is indexing. In an earlier paragraph I referenced the fact that the US censuses have all been indexed, making genealogists' work a lot easier. But there are still *many* records that are just waiting to be indexed – marriage registry books, birth and death registries, funeral home records, baptism and confirmation records, etc. I have been doing genealogy since the days of microfilm records that had no index – so you just scrolled slowly through page after page of microfilmed records in the county you thought your ancestor lived in hopes of finding them. Indexes have made genealogists' research so much easier!

Indexing is quite simple. An indexer goes online and is presented with a digital version of a document. S/he reads the document, and types out the handwritten items before them. That indexer's entry will then be compared with the entry of another indexer. If those two disagree, a third indexer serves as an arbitrator, and determines which, if either, indexer is correct. Here's a caveat, however: Children participating in indexing need to understand and be comfortable with cursive writing. I have worked with a number of teens, helping them learn how to do this, and the younger teens seem to have a more difficult time deciphering older script. Even at that, however, they learn quickly. The knowledge that someone else is interpreting the same document, and that another person then reviews both indexers' work, seems to help them not worry unduly about errors they may be making.

FamilySearch.org always has a need for indexers. If you go to their home page (*www.familysearch.org*), look on the dashboard tray for *Get Involved*. Click that, and one of the choices is *Indexing*. Once on the *Indexing* page, look for the green box labeled *Indexing Help*. Clicking that takes you to a place where you can watch a short, interactive *Guided Tour* tutorial that will give your children (or you!) a pretty good idea of what indexing is, and what is expected of them.

Other organizations are also looking for indexers. I hooked up with a genealogy society in the Arkansas county where my great grandfather was born and lived for a spell. I have been involved in indexing a number of different kinds of that county's records, and have enjoyed it immensely, especially because it feels like I am making a difference in the part of the country from which several lines of my family lived. Doubtless I have indexed documents and records that contain the names of relatives I do not know about — yet. Perhaps it's my great grandmother's brother's wife's family. One day, I may be searching for just that family, and will benefit personally from the indexing work I have done.

Googling

If you have run into a brick wall on a person, couple or family, why not turn to your teen or pre-teen and see if they can spade cyberspace for you in search of these stubborn ancestors of yours? Many young people seem to have a natural intuition when it comes to searching the Internet. Turn them loose to search the Internet, prowl around message boards, peek into genealogical society records, etc. It might surprise you what they can find, and how rapidly they can find it.

Scrapbooking/Photo Albums

My children all seem to have a technology knack that I do not have. A good activity for children is to have them scan old family photos – don't forget your current, immediate family – and put those photos into albums – either physical albums or virtual albums.

Go ahead – relinquish control of those boxes and boxes of photos you've been planning to get to for years, and let your children use their vast technical aptitude to scan the photos and put them in some kind of organized format. You may need to lend a hand on the organization aspects of the work – but even if they only scan all those photos for you, and you do the labeling and organizing, you are hours and hours ahead, and have a project that you both worked on that both of you can be proud of and inspired by once you are finished. And – it's a nice addition to and support for your genealogical research.

Blogging

Even though blogging seems to have lost its appeal from its peak a few years ago, this is an activity that is well within the technical capability of many of today's youth. There are free blogging templates and services out there that are pretty intuitive, even for old guys like me. Have your teenage son or daughter put up a family blog and post pictures of and stories about their ancestors. What a great next step after your teen has gleaned stories and information from his or her grandparents! As of this writing, our daughter still does a family blog – to let the grandparents (my wife and me!) see what's going on in her family. But at the end of each year, she uses Shutterfly to create a print book of their blog that then becomes part of their captured family history.

These are some of the main activities I think are well within the technical capabilities of many of this generation's youth. You know – or will know – the extent of your teen's or preteen's capabilities. To be successful, break them in easy, be available to tutor them, and once they get the swing of things, turn 'em loose – and get out of their way!

Kids & Genealogy Checklist

____Don't forget – with their technical skills, your kids may be fabulous genealogists.

____Start with their parents and grandparents

____Indexing – new collections are coming online every day, and many of them need indexes to be completed. A great opportunity for kids!

____Scrapbooking can be fun, and provide a nice addition to genealogy research. But mentoring may be needed.

____Blogs are still a good way to capture your current family's activities and preserve them for future generations.

Additional Resources

Green, Bob, and Fulford, D. G., *To Our Children's Children: Preserving Family Histories for Generations to Come*, Doubleday Publishing. (March 1993)

Keel, Philipp *All About Me,* Bantam Doubleday Dell Publications. (February 1998)

15

Chat Generative Pre-Trained Transformer (ChatGPT)

You might well be asking yourself: "Can I use ChatGPT to find my ancestors?"

Or, you may be asking yourself: "What is ChatGPT, and can I use it to find my ancestors?"

I'll try to answer both questions. ChatGPT, according to *Wikipedia*, is:

*ChatGPT, which stands for **Chat Generative Pre-trained Transformer**, is a large language model-based chatbot developed by OpenAI and launched on November 30, 2022, which enables users to refine and steer a conversation towards a desired length, format, style, level of detail, and language. Successive prompts and replies, known as prompt engineering, are considered at each conversation stage as a context.*

If you're like me, your response to that definition may well be: "Huh?"

That was still a little unclear to me. I understood most of the words, but wasn't quite certain what they all meant when you put them together – and whether they meant I could use ChatGPT to assist me to find my ancestors. So I turned to a new friend to help me understand what ChatGPT is. My New Friend is: ChatGPT.

That's right – I asked ChatGPT to define itself for me. I went to ChatGPT and asked it this question:

Me: *Define the following definition in language a sixth grader can understand: "ChatGPT, which stands for Chat Generative Pre-trained Transformer, is a large language model-based chatbot developed by OpenAI and launched on November 30, 2022, which enables users to refine and steer a conversation towards a desired length, format, style, level of detail, and language. Successive prompts and replies, known as prompt engineering, are considered at each conversation stage as a context."*

ChatGPT: *Sure! ChatGPT is like a really smart computer friend that helps people have conversations. It's made by a company called OpenAI. Imagine having a helpful buddy that you can talk to and ask questions. You can even tell this computer friend how you want the conversation to be, like how long or detailed you want it to be, and how you want it to sound. It's like having a friend that can talk in different ways, depending on what you like. This computer friend uses fancy technology to understand what you're saying and then respond to you, like having a back-and-forth chat. Each time you say something, it's like adding to a story, and the computer friend keeps track of what's been said to keep the conversation going smoothly.*

ChatGPT uses Artificial Intelligence (AI) to generate responses to questions and carry on conversations, do research, etc. To get to ChatGPT, go to *chat.openai.com/auth/login*. As of this writing, there are two versions of ChatGPT – a free one, and a subscription. The free ChatGPT has been good enough for me. I'm sure as ChatGPT evolves, there will be other AI / ChatGPT-type generators that will become available, all very similar but no doubt adding different features to attract and retain subscribers.

CHAT GENERATIVE PRE-TRAINED TRANSFORMER (CHATGPT)

But for now – try ChatGPT out by going to *chat.openai.com/auth/login* and click the blue *Sign Up* button.

Back to the original question I led with at the outset of this chapter:
"Can I use ChatGPT to find my ancestors?"
My answer would be Yes! And No! Let's see how ChatGPT answers that question:

Me: *Can I use ChatGPT to find my ancestors?*

ChatGPT: *ChatGPT is a text-based AI developed by OpenAI and is not specifically designed to help you find your ancestors. It does not have access to external databases or information about individuals, including genealogical records or family histories.*

To find information about your ancestors, you would typically use genealogical research methods, access relevant records, visit archives, libraries, or use specialized genealogy websites and databases. These sources can provide details about your family history and help you trace your lineage.

If you need assistance with genealogical research or have questions about how to conduct it effectively, you might consider reaching out to a professional genealogist or a genealogy organization for guidance and support.

Okay – so ChatGPT says "No, it can't find individuals" (yet -- I think it has that kind of capability, so perhaps it will be able to do that in the future).

However, it can HELP me find my ancestor (hence my "Yes! Response earlier). I was working with a friend to find a particularly elusive ancestor of his. We'll call her Luronia Smith. I asked ChatGPT this question:

Me: *Can you find Luronia Smith's parents in Bedford, Coffee County,*

Tennessee?

ChatGPT: *I'm unable to browse the internet or access specific, private, or current information about individuals or their family histories. My training only includes information up until September 2021, and I don't have access to genealogical databases or records. If you're looking for genealogical information or trying to trace specific individuals' parents or family histories, I recommend using reputable genealogy websites, local archives, historical records, or consulting a professional genealogist for assistance.*

Rats! But I decided not to give up easily.

Me: *What genealogical resources are available for Bedford, Coffee county, Tennessee?*

Chat GPT: *Genealogical research often involves exploring various resources to trace family history and connections in a specific location. For Bedford and Coffee County, Tennessee, here are some common genealogical resources you may find helpful:*

1. Local Archives and Libraries:
   ***a.** Memorial Library (Bedford County): This library might have local history and genealogical collections relevant to Bedford County.*
   ***b.** Coffee County Lannom Memorial Public Library (Coffee County): Check their local history and genealogy section for resources related to Coffee County.*

2. Historical Societies:
   ***a.** Bedford County Historical Society: Contact them to inquire about genealogical resources, historical records, and publications related to Bedford County.*
   ***b.** Coffee County Historical Society: Inquire about genealogical resources*

and historical records for Coffee County.
3. Online Genealogy Databases:
a. *Ancestry.com:* Ancestry.com often has a wide range of historical records, including census data, vital records, military records, and more that may be relevant to your genealogical research in this area.

b. *FamilySearch.org:* FamilySearch is a free genealogy website that provides access to a vast collection of genealogical records, including census records, vital records, and more.

4. Local Government Offices:
a. Bedford County Clerk's Office: Contact them to inquire about birth, marriage, death records, land records, and other documents relevant to genealogy research.

b. Coffee County Clerk's Office: Check for vital records and other historical documents that might be useful for genealogical research.

5. Cemetery Records:
a. Explore local cemeteries and document tombstone inscriptions. Websites like Find A Grave and BillionGraves can be helpful for locating and documenting graves.

6. Newspapers:
a. Search for historical newspapers in the area, either in local libraries or online archives, to find obituaries, birth announcements, marriage notices, and other relevant information.

7. Local Historical Newspapers:
a. Explore local newspapers that may have archives or historical sections. Examples include "Shelbyville Times-Gazette" for Bedford County and "Manchester Times" for Coffee County.

8. Local Genealogical Societies:
a. Check if there are any local genealogical societies in Bedford or Coffee County. They may have resources, publications, and knowledge about the area's history and genealogy.

Remember to carefully document and cross-reference information obtained from various sources to ensure accuracy in your genealogical research. Additionally, consider reaching out to local experts or genealogists for guidance and further assistance.

Some of those sources may be ones you hadn't thought of as you search for your ancestors – so I stand by my answer that: "Yes! —ChatGPT can help you find your ancestors."

I think ChatGPT may be the newest and most exciting technology for family history research since the Internet became widely available, and since genealogy records became digitized. ChatGPT is still in its infancy, but I am hopeful that it will one day grow and be able to help me – and you — find even the most stubborn and elusive ancestors of mine / yours.

ChatGPT Checklist

____ ChatGPT won't be able to do your genealogical research for you.

____ ChatGPT can recommend specific genealogical sources for you to use while researching your ancestors.

____ ChatGPT may evolve so that it can help you find your ancestors... but right now it is in its infancy. Stay Tuned!

Additional Resources

Verena, Percival C., *The Ultimate Guide to ChatGPT: A Beginner's Handbook to Understanding Engineering, the Future of Artificial Intelligence and How to Use It Effectively*. Publisher: Remington Wahlrab (April 2023)

Haertlein, Glenn, *The ChatGPT Entrepreneur: How to Use ChatGPT to Write Nonfiction, Generate Passive Income, Create Social Media Content, and More*, (September 2023)

Walter, Yohan, *ChatGPT – Learn to use it effectively: From beginner to expert... discover over 150 prompts...to improve your efficiency, save time, and boost your productivity*, (4/2023)

16

In Summary

In writing this book, I have focused on records that you can use to begin your genealogy adventure — right now! I did not want to overwhelm you with large dollops of information, but I did want to give you some tools, records, and direction to ease you into this Great Obsession, so you could be successful in your ancestral search right away.

If your experience is like mine, this will be the beginning of a life-long adventure that will bring you a great deal of satisfaction, and introduce you to new friends and long-lost cousins. It may even take you to far-flung corners of the world, either via the Internet or in person, in search of your roots.

Below are the high points to remember when you begin your genealogical journey:

- Start with what you know.
- Expand to find out what your relatives know.
- Vital records include birth, death, and marriage information. Obtaining documentation of these events should be one of your main goals as a researcher.

- The Internet is one of the greatest aids to genealogical research ever. The click of a mouse may help you learn information that has eluded you for years in your genealogical research.
- Census records provide a wealth of information about your ancestors. Remember, however, that they are secondary sources, but can help lead you to primary sources.
- Immigration and naturalization records can yield a ton of marvelous genealogical information if you have immigrant ancestors.
- Military records are an often-overlooked source of genealogical information.

If you have found this book helpful, I would appreciate it if you would go on Amazon.com and leave a favorable review. **However** — on the other hand, if you found it lacking, I'd prefer for you to please let me know at *wdanielquillen@gmail.com*. I always welcome input that comes directly to me, particularly when I have overlooked something, or have written a section that was confusing or unclear. I often incorporate that input into future editions of my books. Also — if you have research questions I can help you with, reach out to me at that e-mail address as well. Through the years, I have provided one-on-one research help to literally hundreds of my readers (my friends!). It brings me great joy to do that, so please don't hesitate to reach out.

And finally — once you embark on this path to who you are and where you came from, you are in for a treat indeed. May it be all you hope it will be. It has been so for me.

17

Resources

Ancestry® | *Family Tree, genealogy & Family History Records.* (n.d.). www.ancestry.com/

CyndisList.com — Ingle, C. (n.d.). *Welcome to Cyndi's list.* Copyright (C) 1996-2022 Cyndi Ingle. All Rights Reserved. This Site May Be Freely Linked to but Not Duplicated in Any Fashion Without My Consent. Graphics Property of Cyndi Ingle. https://cyndislist.com/

FamilySearch.org. (2023, September 1). FamilySearch.org. Retrieved September 25, 2023, from www.familysearch.org

Find a grave - millions of cemetery records. (n.d.). www.findagrave.com

Findmypast. (n.d.). *Find your ancestors & family history - Genealogy & Ancestry - Findmypast.co.uk.* www.findmypast.com/

Fold3 - Historical military records. (n.d.). Fold3. www.fold3.com/

Free family tree, genealogy, family history, and DNA testing. (n.d.). MyHeritage. www.myheritage.com/

National Archives |. (n.d.). www.archives.gov/

National Genealogical Society, www.NGSGenealogy.org

Newspapers.com find your news about your ancestors — births, deaths, marriages, obituaries, etc.

RAOGK - Random Acts of Genealogical Kindness. (2020, May 5).

www.raogk.org/

The Civil War (U.S. National Park Service). https://nps.gov/civilwar

Notice: FamilySearch is a registered trademark of Intellectual Reserve, Inc.

All photos used, including the front cover photo and interior photos, are the property of Daniel Quillen.

18

Praise for Quillen's Other Genealogy Books

"Quillen's *Secrets of Tracing Your Ancestors* shows those new to the hobby how to begin their genealogy, while showing seasoned family historians some new tricks. Covering the basics such as organization, the best genealogical websites, and how to do family group sheets. Quillen approaches the subject with passion and a touch of humor." — *Family Chronicle* magazine

"Of all the books I have looked at, yours is the best...and you write with your heart and soul. Thanks for writing such a great book." — Karen Dredge

"Thanks for your help and for writing your excellent book!" – Laura Johnson

"It is not only informative but entertaining...thank you for helping me to understand the many aspects of genealogy and for supplying a roadmap to finding more information about our ancestors." – Dana L. Hager

"I got your book out of the library, but before I was half-way through it, I decided I had to have my own copy. Lots of helpful suggestions! I'd recommend it for new and experienced family historians." – Margaret Combs

"I am researching my family genealogy and had trouble with locating records of those members who had immigrated from Germany. This book was what I needed. It made it possible for me to locate those members who were so elusive. I definitely recommend it as a great resource for anyone experiencing the same problem." — Jilane

"Quillen's genealogical guides are the best!" – Cynthia and Michael Fields

"If you need help with your genealogy research turn to this author, Daniel Quillen. He explains the how-to steps of searching for those ancestors hiding in the records available online. All his books are super helpful." – CJ

"Had to drop you a note and let you know how much my students LOVE your books ... You are a wonderful writer! One of the things my students really love is that it is like sitting down with a friend and talking. So much fun! ... I love it ... So glad I have your books to offer them!! DON'T STOP WRITING!!" J. Sopko (Community College Genealogy class instructor about *Quillen's Essentials of Genealogy* series)

19

Quillen's Other Books

Secrets of Tracing Your Ancestors
Troubleshooter's Guide to Do-It-Yourself Genealogy
Quillen's Essential Genealogy series:
Mastering Online Genealogy
Mastering Immigration and Naturalization Records
Mastering Census and Military Records
Tracing Your European Ancestors
Tracing Your Irish and British Ancestors
Mastering Family, Library and Church Records
Get a Job!
The Perfect Resume
The Perfect Interview
Your First Job
Use Social Media to Find Your Dream Job (co-authored with Dr. Lance Farr)

20

About the Author

For the past two+ decades, W. Daniel Quillen has been a professional writer specializing in travel and technical subjects. He has taught beginning genealogy courses to university students and working adults, and is a frequent lecturer in beginning and intermediate genealogy classes in Colorado and at regional genealogical conferences. His genealogy books have even been featured on the hit television show NCIS (March 2018)! He has compiled his years of genealogical training and research into nine genealogy books, including his latest effort: *Beginner's Guide to Genealogy* – a concise tutorial for beginning genealogists.

He lives in Castle Rock, Colorado with his wife, and spends much of his discretionary time and money visiting his (six children and) eighteen grandchildren, most of whom live coast to coast! If you would like to contact him about anything in this book, his e-mail address is wdanielquillen@gmail.com.

Printed in Great Britain
by Amazon